The BiG BooK OF CATS

THE BIG BOOK OF CATS

FUN FACTS, FASCINATING ANECDOTES, AND QUOTATIONS ABOUT FELINES

EDITED BY SUSAN FEUER

ILLUSTRATED BY ANA CIÇA PINTO

Gramercy Books

New York

This 2000 edition is published by Gramercy Books™,
an imprint of Random House Value Publishing, Inc.,
280 Park Avenue, New York, New York 10017,
by arrangement with Andrews McMeel Publishing.

Gramercy Books™ and design are trademarks of
Random House Value Publishing, Inc.

Random.House
New York • Toronto • London • Sydney • Auckland
http://www.randomhouse.com/

Printed and bound in the United States of America

Library of Congress Cataloging-in-Publication Data

The big book of cats : fun facts, fascinating anecdotes, and
quotations about felines / edited by Susan Feuer.
        p. cm.
   Originally published: Kansas City, MO : Andrews McMeel
Pub., c1998.
   ISBN 0-517-16186-9
      1. Cats—Miscellanea. I. Feuer, Susan.

SF445.5 .B54 2000
636.8—dc21

                                                        00-057675

8 7 6 5 4 3 2 1

The writers (and the cats who love them) for The Big Book of Cats are: Karen Liljedahl (Candy and Wally), Paul Lipari (Nicole), Patricia Cronin Marcello (Draco, Pearl, and Zuzy), Catherine Murphy (Bumblebee and Panda), Joan Schweighardt (Sammie and Speedy Clark), Carolyn Short (Butterfinger and Tiger), Mitchell Uscher (Ceil and Flakey), and Daniel R. White (Lucy, Sylvia, and Willie).

CONTENTS

INTRODUCTION

You love cats. It's that simple.

More than mere pets, they are companions, friends, and confidants. They are your babies, your children. Your cat—or cats— have you wrapped around their paws. Felines rule your life, which is just fine with you. In fact, you wouldn't want it any other way. This book is written for you and your fellow cat fanciers. From quotations to cat care tips, from the history of the feline to descriptions of breeds, from little-known facts to fun anecdotes, it's in here. And lots more! So curl up on the couch with you-know-who and read on about these wonderful, special creatures.

KITTY QUIPS: SOME CAT QUOTATIONS

If cats could talk, they
wouldn't.

—*Nan Porter*

The problem with cats is that
they get the exact same look on
their face whether they see a
moth or an ax-murderer.

—*Paula Poundstone*

Cats are absolute individuals,
with their own ideas about
everything, including the
people they own.
          —John Dingman

If stretching were
wealth, the cat would
be rich.
          —African proverb

It is easy to understand why
the rabble dislike cats. A cat is
beautiful; it suggests ideas of
luxury, cleanliness, voluptuous
pleasures.
          —Charles Baudelaire

A kitten is chiefly remarkable
for rushing about like mad at
nothing whatever, and generally stopping before it gets
there.

—*Agnes Repplier*

A dog is a dog, a bird is a bird,
and a cat is a person.

—*Mugsy Peabody*

When a Cat adopts you there
is nothing to be done about it
except to put up with it and
wait until the wind changes.

—*T. S. Eliot*

Living with a cat is like being
married to a career woman who
can take domesticity or let it
alone, so you'd better be nice
to her.
                    —*Margaret Cooper Gay*

A cat can purr its way out of
anything.
                    —*Donna McCrohan*

Cats seldom make mistakes,
and they never make the same
mistake twice.
                    —*Carl Van Vechten*

As soon as they're out of your sight, you are out of their mind.
—*Walter de la Mare*

All animals are equal, but some animals are more equal than others.
—*George Orwell*

We should be careful to get out
of an experience only the wis-
dom that is in it—and stop
there; lest we be like the cat
that sits on a hot stove lid. She
will never sit down on a hot
stove lid again—and that is
well; but also she will never sit
down on a cold one anymore.
—Mark Twain

Because his long,
white whiskers tick-
led, I began every
day laughing.
—Janet F. Faure

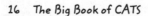

I called my cat William because no shorter name fits the dignity of his character. Poor old man, he has fits now, so I call him fitz-William.

—*Josh Billings*

There is no more intrepid explorer than a kitten.

—*Jules Champfleury*

Those who'll play with cats must expect to be scratched.

—*Miguel de Cervantes*

*E*verything that moves serves to interest and amuse a cat. He is convinced that nature is busying herself with his diversion; he can conceive of no other purpose in the universe.

—F. A. *Paradis de Moncrif*

*C*ats must have three names— an everyday name, such as Peter; a more particular, dignified name, such as Quaxo, Bombalurina, or Jellylorum; and, thirdly, the name the cat thinks up for himself, his deep and inscrutable singular Name.

—*T. S. Eliot*

We quickly discovered that
two kittens were
much more fun
than one.
—*Allen Lacy*

Old cats mean young mice.
—*Italian proverb*

The way to keep a cat is to try
to chase it away.
—*E. W. Howe*

Dogs come when they're
called; cats take a message and
get back to you.
—*Mary Bly*

I am indebted to the species of
the cat for a particular kind of
honorable deceit, for a great
control over myself, for characteristic aversion to brutal
sounds, and for the need to
keep silent for long periods of
time.

—*Colette*

Cats are only human, they
have their faults.

—*Kingsley Amis*

A sleeping cat is ever alert.

—*Fred Schwab*

The cat has too much spirit to have no heart.
>—Ernest Menault

If a fish is the movement of water embodied, given shape, then a cat is a diagram and pattern of subtle air.
>—Doris Lessing

It is in their eyes that their magic resides.
>—Arthur Symons

A mouse in the paws is worth two in the pantry.
>—Louis Wain

Of all animals, he alone attains the Contemplative Life. He regards the wheel of existence from without, like the Buddha. There is no pretense of sympathy about the cat. He lives alone, aloft, sublime, in a wise passiveness.

—*Andrew Lang*

"It's going to freeze," she would say, "the cat's dancing."

—*Colette*

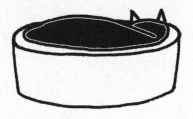

If animals could speak, the dog would be a blundering, outspoken, honest fellow—but the cat would have the rare grace of never saying a word too much.

—*Philip Gilbert Hamerton*

Even the stupidest cat seems to know more than any dog.

—*Eleanor Clark*

A cat sneezing is a good omen for everyone who hears it.

—*Italian superstition*

Another cat? Perhaps. For love
there is also a season;
its seeds must be re-
sown. But a family cat is
not replaceable like a
worn-out coat or a set of
tires. Each new kitten
becomes its own cat,
and none is repeated. I
am four cats old, measur-
ing out my life in friends that
have succeeded but not replaced one another.
                    —Irving Townsend

The cat is utterly sincere.
                    —Fernand Méry

If you want to be a psychological novelist and write about
human beings, the best thing
you can do is keep a pair of
cats.

—*Aldous Huxley*

Cat: A pygmy lion who loves
mice, hates dogs, and patron-
izes human beings.

—*Oliver Herford*

If a dog jumps up into your lap,
it is because he is fond of you;
but if a cat does the same
thing, it is because your lap is
warmer.

—*Alfred North Whitehead*

A cat sleeping with all four paws tucked under means cold weather ahead.

—*English superstition*

The cat has always been associated with the Moon. Like the Moon it comes to life at night, escaping from humanity and wandering over housetops with its eyes beaming out through the darkness.

—*Patricia Dale-Green*

Two cats can live as cheaply as one, and their owner has twice as much fun.

—*Lloyd Alexander*

A cat is never vulgar.
> —*Carl Van Vechten*

*I*t [the Cheshire Cat] vanished quite slowly, beginning with the end of the tail, and ending with the grin, which remained some time after the rest of it had gone.
> —*Lewis Carroll*

A home without a cat—and a well-fed, well-petted, and properly revered cat—may be a perfect home, perhaps, but how can it prove its title?
> —*Mark Twain*

Cats seem to go on the prin-
ciple that it never does any
harm to ask for what you want.
—Joseph Wood Krutch

Should ever anything be
missed—milk, coals, umbrellas,
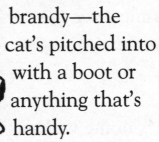 brandy—the
cat's pitched into
with a boot or
anything that's
handy.
—C. S. Calverley

Cats mean kittens, plentiful
and frequent.
—Doris Lessing

Pure herring oil is the port
wine of English cats.

                 —Honoré de Balzac

It is impossible for a lover of
cats to banish these alert,
gentle, and discriminating
friends, who give us just
enough of their regard and
complaisance to make us
hunger for more.

                 —Agnes Repplier

Cleanliness in the cat world is
usually a virtue put above god-
liness.

                 —Carl Van Vechten

*U*nlike us, cats never outgrow
their delight in cat capacities,
nor do they settle finally for
limitations. Cats, I think, live
out their lives fulfilling their
expectations.

—*Irving Townsend*

*C*ats are notoriously sore
losers. Coming in second best,
especially to someone as poorly
coordinated as a human being,
grates their sensibility.

—*Stephen Baker*

*N*o one can have experienced
to the fullest the true sense of
achievement and satisfaction
who has never pursued
and successfully caught
his tail.
>—*Rosalind Welcher*

*A*n old cat will not
learn dancing.
>—*Moroccan proverb*

I shall never forget the indulgence with which he treated Hodge, his cat, for whom he used to go out and buy oysters, lest the servants having that trouble should take a dislike to the poor creature. . . . I recol-

lect him one day scrambling up on Dr. Johnson's breast, apparently with much satisfaction, while my friend, smiling and half-whistling, rubbed his back and pulled him by the tail; and when I observed he was a fine cat, saying, "Why, yes, Sir, but I have had cats whom I liked better than this." And then as if perceiving Hodge to be out of countenance, adding, "But he is a very fine cat, a very fine cat indeed."

—*James Boswell*

Her function is to sit and be admired.
—*Georgina Strickland Gates*

The cat does not offer services. The cat offers itself. Of course he wants care and shelter. You don't buy love for nothing. Like all pure creatures, cats are practical.
—*William S. Burroughs*

The more you rub a cat on the rump, the higher she sets her tail.

—*John Ray*

Way down deep, we're all mo-
tivated by the same urges. Cats
have the courage to live by
them.

—*Jim Davis*

If only cats grew
into kittens.

—*R. D. Stern*

Cats always know whether
people like or dislike them.
They do not always care
enough to do anything about it.

—*Winifred Carriere*

Cats are smarter than dogs.
You can't get eight cats to pull
a sled through snow.

—Jeff Valdez

When the cat and mouse
agree, the grocer is ruined.

—*Iranian proverb*

A black cat dropped sound-
lessly from a high wall, like a
spoonful of dark treacle, and
melted under a gate.
—*Elizabeth Lemarchand*

*T*he ideal of calm exists in a
sitting cat.
—*Jules Reynard*

*T*hey say the test of literary
power is whether a man can
write an inscription. I say, "Can
he name a kitten?"
—*Samuel Butler*

*C*ats are designated friends.
—*Norman Corwin*

VERSES ON THE CAT: A SELECTION OF POETRY

Cats are a mysterious kind of
  folk—
there is more passing in their
  minds
than we are aware of.
                    —*Sir Walter Scott*

The Kilkenny Cats

There wanst was two cats of
  Kilkenny.
And aich thought there was
  wan cat too many;
So they quarrelled and fit,
And they scratched and they
  bit,
Till barin' their nails
And the tips of their tails,
Instead of two cats, there
  warn't any.

—*Anonymous*

Let take a cat, and foster him
    well with milk
And tender flesh and make his
    couch of silk,
And let him seen a mouse go
    by the wall,
Anon he waveth milk and flesh
    and all,
And every dainty that is in that
    house,
Such appetite he hath to eat a
    mouse.

    —*Geoffrey Chaucer*

She sights a Bird—she
    chuckles—
She flattens—then she
    crawls—
She runs without the look of
    feet—
Her eyes increase to Balls.
                    —*Emily Dickinson*

As I was going to St. Ives,
I met a man with seven wives,
Each wife had seven sacks,
Each sack has seven cats,
Each cat had seven kits:
Kits, cats, sacks, wives,
How many were going to St.
   Ives?
                    —*Nursery rhyme*

Verses on a Cat

A cat in distress,
Nothing more, nor less;
Good folks, I must faithfully
   tell ye,
As I am a sinner,
It waits for some dinner

To stuff out its own little belly.

You would not easily guess
All the modes of distress
Which torture the tenants of
    earth;
And the various evils,
Which like so many devils,
Attend the poor souls from
    their birth.

Some a living require,
And others desire
An old fellow out of the way;
And which is the best
I leave to be guessed,
For I cannot pretend to say.

One wants society,
Another variety,
Others a tranquil life;
Some want food.
Others, as good,
Only want a wife.

But this poor little cat
Only wanted a rat,
To stuff out its own little maw;
And it were as good
Some people had such food,
To make them hold their jaw.

—Percy Bysshe Shelley

One is tabby with emerald
  eyes,
And a tail that's long and
  slender,
And into a temper she quickly
  flies
If you ever by chance offend
  her.

—*Thomas Hood*

Two little kittens, one stormy
    night,
Began to quarrel, and then to
    fight;
One had a mouse, the other
    had none,
And that's the way the quarrel
    begun.

                    —*Anonymous*

To a Cat

Stately, kindly, lordly friend,
Condescend
Here to sit by me, and turn
Glorious eyes that smile and
   burn,
Golden eyes, love's lustrous
   meed,
On the golden page I read.

All your wondrous wealth of
  hair,
Dark and fair,
Silken-shaggy, soft and bright
As the clouds and beams of
  night,
Pays my reverent hand's caress
Back with friendlier gentleness.

Dogs may fawn on all and some
As they come;
You, a friend of loftier mind,
Answer friends alone in kind.
Just your foot upon my hand
Softly bids it understand.
                —Algernon Swinburne

Pussy will rub my knees with
    her head
Pretending she loves me hard;
But the very minute I go to bed
Pussy runs out in the yard . . .
                    —*Rudyard Kipling*

Who's that ringing at my door-
    bell?
A little pussy cat that isn't very
    well.
Rub its little nose with a little
    mutton fat,
That's the best cure for a little
    pussy cat.
                    —*Nursery rhyme*

Dearest cat, honoured guest of
    my old house,
Arch your supple, tingling
    back,
And curl upon my knee, to let
    me
Bathe my fingers in your warm
    fur.

—François Lemaître

The cat went here and there
And the moon spun round like
   a top,
And the nearest kin of the
   moon,
The creeping cat, looked up.
Black Minnaloushe stared at
   the moon,
For, wander and wail as he
   would,
The pure cold light in the sky
Troubled his animal blood.
Minnaloushe runs in the grass
Lifting his delicate feet.
Do you dance, Minnaloushe,
   do you dance?
                    —William Butler Yeats

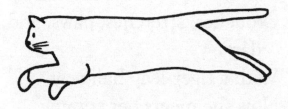

The Kitten at Play

See the kitten on the wall,
Sporting with the leaves that
  fall,
Withered leaves, one, two, and
  three
Falling from the elder tree,
Through the calm and frosty
  air
Of the morning bright and fair.

See the kitten, how she starts,
Crouches, stretches, paws, and
    darts;
With a tiger-leap half way
Now she meets her coming
    prey.
Lets it go as fast and then
Has it in her power again.

Now she works with three and
    four,
Like an Indian conjurer;
Quick as he in feats of art,
Gracefully she plays her part;
Yet were gazing thousands
    there,
What would little Tabby care?
            —*William Wordsworth*

Bathsheba:
To whom none ever said scat,
No worthier cat
Ever sat on a mat
Or caught a rat:
Requies-cat.
—*John Greenleaf Whittier*

Pussy cat, pussy cat,
Where have you been?
I've been to London
To look at the Queen.
Pussy cat, pussy cat,
What did you there?
I frightened a little mouse
Under her chair.
—*Nursery rhyme*

Sonnet to Mrs. Reynolds' Cat

Cat! who hast pass'd thy grand
    climacteric,
How many mice and rats hast
    in thy days
Destroy'd—How many tid-bits
    stolen? Gaze
With those bright languid seg-
    ments green, and prick
Those velvet ears—but
    pr'ythee do not stick
Thy latent talons in me—and
    upraise
Thy gentle mew—and tell me
    all thy frays
Of fish and mice, and rats and
    tender chick.

Nay, look not down, nor lick
thy dainty wrists—
    For all the wheezy
        asthma—and for all
        Thy tail's tip is
            nick'd off—and
            though the fists
            Of many a maid
            have given thee
    many a maul,
Still is that fur as soft as when
    the lists
In youth thou enter'dst on glass
    bottled wall.
                    —*John Keats*

Dame Trot and her cat
Sat down for a chat;
The Dame sat on this side
And puss sat on that.

Puss, says the Dame
Can you catch a rat
Or a mouse in the dark?
Purr, says the cat.

—Nursery rhyme

But buds will be roses,
and kittens, cats,
—more's the pity.

—Louisa May Alcott

Ding, dong, bell
Pussy's in the well.
Who put her in?
Little Johnny Green.
Who pulled her out?
Little Tommy Stout.
What a naughty boy was that
To try to drown poor pussy cat,
Who never did him any harm,
And killed the mice in his
    father's barn.

—*Nursery rhyme*

Six little mice sat down to spin;
Pussy passed by and she peeped
   in.
What are you doing, my little
   men?
Weaving coats for gentlemen.
Shall I come in and cut off your
   threads?
No, no, Mistress Pussy, you'd
   bite off our heads.
On, no, I'll not; I'll help you to
   spin.
That may be so, but don't you
   come in.

—*Nursery rhyme*

WHAT TO NAME A CAT

GENERAL, ALL-PURPOSE, UNDIFFERENTIATED CATS; OR, CATS FOR ALL SEASONS

Abby

Abyssinian

Algernon

Angora

Arizona

Blitz

Boise

Bolo

Boots

Boro

Bose
Box
Budge
Buff
Burma
Bush, Bushy
Calcutta
Captain
Casca
Checkers
Chickens
Cincy
Courtesan
Crossword
Domino
Egbert
Eliot
Esperanto

France
Gateway
Goldilocks
Gypsy
Halifax
Heliotrope
Herman
Hermione
Holy Smoke
Hyacinth
Jellybean
Jodhpur
Lafcadio
Lafitte
Lobo
Lord Saville
Louis
Luigi

Lynx
Magic
Mantelpiece
Marmaduke
Max Factor
Midnight
Muff

Mulligan
Mystery
Pajamas
Peggy
Piggy
Playboy
Playgirl
Pumpkin
Rainbow
Rupert
Sax
Scoop
Scrabble
Seabrook
Silas
Simon
Slick Willie
Smokey

Spinner

Strand

Tabby

Tabitha

Tarantella

Tickee

Tig

Tiger

Tiger Woods

Ultramarine

Valerian

Vesper

Vixen

Webster

Whisper

Willows

Zoney

ADVENTUROUS
AND
EXPLORATORY
CATS

Amazon

Amerigo

Audubon.

Ayesha

Captain Cook

Catlin

Chardin

Clark

Columbus

Coronado

Cortez

Dr. Livingston

Hakluyt

Lewis
Lhasa
Mandeville
Nile
Pathfinder
Quatermain
Rider

Rider Haggard
Sir Richard
   Burton
Stanley
Stargazer
Starman
Tartary
Trailblazer
Vasco
Yucatán

ARTISTICATS

Bernini
Bosch
Botticelli
Cassatt
Cellini

Chiaroscuro   Modigliani
De Chirico   Monet
Dürer   Munch
El Greco   Phydias
Fragonard   Picasso
Giotto   Picatso
Goya   Piranesi
Hieronymous   Poussin
Hokusai   Raeburn
Kokoschka   Raphael
Laurencin   Rembrandt
     Renoir
     Reubens
     Ririomin
     Rothko
     Sargent
Leonardo   Schiele
Michelangelo   Silkscreen

Tintoretto
Titian
Turner
Velásquez
Vermeer
Veronese
Watteau
Whistler
Zurbarán

CINEMATI-
CATS

Al
Antonioni
Astaire
Avenger
Baby

Bergman
Blore
Bogart
Bogey, Bogie
Brando
Buster Keaton
Cary Grant
Casablanca
Chaplin

Christie
Citizen Kane
Coop
De Niro
Diana Rigg
Dino
Dr. No
Dr. Phibes
Eastwood
Fat Man
Federico
Fred
Ginger
Godfrey

Harvey
Hepburn
Hollywood
Holly Wood
Hopkins
Irene
Jack
Joan Fontaine
Judy Garland
Kurosawa
La Brea
Lancaster
Lombard
Maltese Falcon
Mansfield
Max de
  Winter
Merkin Muffley

Michael Caine   Sean Connery
Minnelli   Sierra Madre
Mizoguchi   Sinatra
Mrs. Peel   Spielberg
Nicholson   Steed
Olivier   Sunset
Oscar   Swing Time
Ozu   Titanic
Pacino   Top Hat
Paradise   Vine
Peck   Welles
Perry Mason
Powell   CLASSICATS
Rat Pack   AND
Rebecca   MYTHICATS
Russell
Sam   Aeschylus
Sam Spade   Agamemnon

Ajax

Alcibiades

Alexander

Alexandria

Anaximander

Antony

Apollo

Argo

Aristotle

Brutus

Caesar

Castor

Cicero

Circe

Clytemnestra

Colosseo

Cressida

Croesus

Cupid

Cyclops

Daedalus

Diana

Emperor

Euripides

Fury

Hecate

Hector

Helen

Heraclitus

Hercules

Hermes

Herodotus

Homer

Horace

Icarus

Kato

Janus
Julius
Justinian
Marc Antony
Morpheus
Narcissus
Nero
Octavian
Odysseus
Orestes
Orpheus
Ovid
Pan
Pericles
Plato
Plutarch
Pollux
Praxiteles

Prometheus
Psyche
Rubicon
Sallust
Seneca
Socrates
Sophocles
Tacitus
Telemachus
Terence
Tiber
Tiburon
Trajan
Troilus
Ulysses
Virgil

DICKENSICATS

Artful Dodger	Dorrit
Blimber	Drood
Boffin	Estella
Boythorn	Fagin
Boz	Fezziwig
Bumble	Florence
Chuzzle	Grip
Chuzzlewit	Guppy
Copperfield	Havisham
Cratchit	Heep
Cricket	Jaggers
Cuttle	Jarndyce
Datchery	Jasper
Dedlock	Jellyby
Dickens	Jingle
Dombey	Lady Dedlock
	Little Nell
	Little Dorrit

Magwitch
Marley
Master
  Humphrey
Meagles
Micawber
Miss Flite
Mudfog
Nell
Nipper
Noggs
Oliver
Pecksniff
Peggotty
Phiz
Pickwick
Pip
Quilp

Raven
Sapsea
Skimpole
Squeers
Swiveller
Sikes
Tigg
Tiny Tim
Todgers
Tox, Toxie
Trot
Twist

Varden
Wemmick

DINOCATS

Alamo
Alioram
Allosore
Anato
Anchi
Ankylo
Bactro
Baryo
Brachy
Bronto
Camaro
Campto
Ceratty

Cetiosaur
Compy
Daspy
Deino
Dimetri
Dinocat
Dippy
Dromy
Dryo
Galli
Godzilla
Godzo
Hadro
Iguano
Jurassicat
Kentro
Krito
Lambeo

Longsiquam   Stego
Magalo   T. Rex
Maia   Tarbo
Nodo   Torosaur
Notho   Triassicat
Othnie   Vectio
Ovi   Velosso
Pachy
Placo   *EDUCATED*
Plateo   *PUSSIES*
Pterry
Quetzal   Barnard
Rapto   Biblicat
Scutello   Boss Cat
Scuto   Boss Tweed
Siluro   Brown
Sordy   Bryn Mawr
Spiny   Columbia

Cornell
Dartmouth
Dr. Seuss
Dr. Katz
Duke
Educat
Harvard
Ivy
Ivy League
Latinicat
Lehigh
Numquam
Numcat
Philosophicat
Princeton
Professor
Quid
Radcliffe

Runecat
Scientificat
Smith
Stanford
Swarthmore
Vassar
Villanova
Wasteland
Wellesley
Yale

FOREIGN CATS

Cattus (Latin)
Chat (French)
Féline
(French)
Feles

Felis (Latin)

Felino (Spanish)

Fellini

Gato (Spanish and Portuguese)

Gatto (Italian)

Katze (German)

Kissa (Finnish)

Minnaloushe

Minou

Neko (Japanese)

Reynard

FUTURE AND FANTASTICATS

1984

Aldiss

Alien

Andromeda

Ballard

Beetlejuice

Dot Com

Droid

Eldritch

Fritz Lang

Futuro

Gormenghast

H. G.

Huxley

Internet

Lao Wells
Mars Wyndham
Memison X-Cat
Mezentian X-Tro
Mulder
Omni HISTORICATS
Orwell
Ouroboros Aaron Burr
Pluto Agricola
Robo Agrippa
Rocky Horror Aguirre
Scully Albertus
SF Magnus
Sigourney Alchemy
Timeslip Alembic
Toffler Alexander
Venus Nevsky
Viriconium Anastasia

Assyria
Avicenna
Aztec
Bligh
Bonaparte
Borgia
Browne
Burgundy
Burr

Catherine   Darnton
Charlemagne   Darwin
Clausewitz   Dastin
Constantine   Dee
Copernicus   Elizabeth I
Cosimo   Flamel
Czar Nicholas   Fosse
Darius   Gregory
Darnley   Hamilton

Hannibal
Inca
Jacobin
Jefferson
Justinian
Lenin
Lincoln
Lucrezia
Marathon
Marco Polo
Marx
Maya
Medici
Napoleon
Newton
Nicholas
Patton
Phoenicia

Quincy
Rasputin
Robespierre
Rommel
Salamis
Savanarola
Spartan
Trojan
Trotsky
Vlad

LITERARY
CATS, ENGLISH
AND
AMERICAN

Aiken
Alice

Amelia	Burns
Arden	Byron
Aspern	Byzantium
Austen	Carlyle
Baldwin	Carwin
Balthazar	Changeling
Basil	Chesterfield
Basil Seal	Childe Harold
Beckford	Clarissa
Beerbohm	Clea
Ben Bulben	Clinker
Benson	Colin
Beocat	Congreve
Beowulf	Conrad
Bertie	Dahl
Branwell	Daisy
Brontë	Darcy
Burgess	De Quincey

Defoe
Dickens
Dido
Dodo
Don Juan
Dorian Grey
Dryden
Duchess
Ecben
Edgeworth
Emma

Ethan
Etherege
Fanny Hill
Fata Morgana
Feversham
Fielding
Fitzwilliam
Frome
Gatsby
Gaunt
George Eliot
Gorboduc
Gore
Gulliver
Hawthorne
Heathcliff
Herrick
Ingersoll

Jane	Maisie
Jane Austen	Malcolm
Jane Eyre	Malfi
Jeeves	Malmsey
Jonathan Wild	Mapp
Joseph	Marlowe
Andrews	Maud Gonne
Jurgen	Maugham
Justine	Melville
Keats	Millay
Kipling	Milton
Kit	Mountolive
Kotzwinkle	Mrs. Dalloway
Lewis Carroll	Mr. Mulline
Lizzy Bennet	Mulliner
Lovelace	Nabokov
Lowry	Naipaul
Lucia	Noël Coward

Northanger   of course, is
Old Possum   silent)
Orlando   Queeg
Ormond   Quincy
Oscar   Quint
Oswald   Radcliffe
Otranto   Rasselas
Pale Fire   Rochester
Pamela   Rushdie
Peacock   Sackville
Pepys   Saki
Peter Quint   Santayana
Pinfold   Sapphira
Pope   Shamela
Powell   Shandy
Poynton   Shaw
Prufrock   Shelley
Psmith (the *p*,   Sheridan

Somerset
Sterne
Swift
Theroux
Trilby
Trollope
Truman
Ustinov
Vathek
Verlock
Vernon
Vidal
Villette
Virginia Woolf
Volpone
Walpole
Waugh
Wharton

White Devil
Wieland
Wildfell
Wilkes
Wilkie
Wodehouse
Wooster
Wycherley
Wylder
Wyvern
Xanadu

Yeats
Zelda
Zuleika

LITERARY
CATS,
WORLDWIDE

Ada
Albertine
Anna
  Karenina
Balzac
Baudelaire
Bovary
Broch
Candide
Canute

Cazotte
Céline
Chekhov
D'Annunzio
Decamerone
Dosto
Dostoevsky
Dr. Faustus
Effi Briest
Ferdydurke
Flaubert
Flea
Fléa
Formica
Franz Kafka
Genet
Genji
Gogol

Golem   Maupin
Gombrowicz   Meyrink
Hamsun   Mirbeau
Heimito   Munchausen
Hippocrene   Murasaki
Hoffmann   Musil
Jung   Natasha
Justine   Odin
Kleist   Pico
Koestler   Pierre
Krespel   Pillow Book
Lady Murasaki   Pirandello
Leopardi   Proust
Loki   Pushkin
Lolita   Quixote
Madeleine   Rabelais
Manzoni   Ragnarok
Marrakesh   Sancho Panza

Saragossa Verga
Schnitzler Zhivago
Sei Shonagon
Senso MEDIEVAL
Sheherazade AND
Simplicissimus ARTHURIAN
Smarra CATS
Smilla
Sposa Aucassin
Stavrogin Bedevere
Stendhal Blamor
Strindberg Bleoberis
Thor Bragwaine
Tocqueville Brandegoris
Tolstoy Camelot
Turgenev Caxton
Unamuno Chaucer
Valéry Clariance

Dagonet

El Cid

Eliazer

Evelake

Galahad, Sir

Gareth

Gawain

Graal

Griflet

Gringamore

Guinevere

Isolde

King Arthur

Lamorak, Sir

Lancelot, Sir

Lanceor

Langland

Lavaine

Lionors

Listinoise

Logris

Lynet

Lyonesse

Malory

Meliagaunt

Meliodas

Merlin

Mondrains

Mordred

Morgan Le
Fay

Nacien

Ontzlake

Ozana

Palomides

Parzival, Percival

Pearl	Bach
Pellam	Ballo
Pelleas	Banjo
Pellinor	Bartók
Piers	Beethoven
Priamus	Berlioz
Roland	Bix
Sadok	Bizet
Sagramore	Camille
Sangrail	Carmen
Tristan	Cello
	Chopin
MUSICATS	Clara
	Clavier
Allegro	Cole Porter
Amadeus	Conga
Aria	Czardas
Aubade	Damper

Dancer
Dinu
Dvorak
Elise

Ella
Ellington
Fauré

Foxtrot
Frank
Fugue
Gamba
Gershwin
Grieg
Haydn
Intermezzo
Johann
  Sebastian
Kreutzer
Krumhorn
Legato
Liszt
Ludwig Van
Mancini
Mercer
Moonlight

Motet

Mozart

Narcisco

Nocturne

Offenbach

Operetta

Orfeo

Paderewski

Paganini

Passacaglia

Pink Panther

Pizzicatta

Prokofiev

Puccini

Quintet

Rachmaninoff

Ravel

Rhapsody

Rhumba

Ritornello

Rossini

Saint-Saëns

Salieri

Satch

Scarlatti

Schubert

Schumann

Scriabine

Sibelius

Sinatra

Sinistra

Smetana

Sonata

Sonatina

Stafford

Stave

Strad

Stradivarius

Straus

Stravinski

Symphonetta

Tannhäuser

Tarantella

Telemann

Toccata

Toscanini

Tremolo

Trout

Verdi

Viola

Wagner

MYSTERIOUS
AND
SUPERNATURAL
CATS

Agatha

Algernon

Algiz

Anne Rice

Armadale

Asphyx

Atlantis
Basil
Baskerville
Bast
Bastet
Bathory
Bedlam
Benito Cereno
Biggers
Blackwood
Bram
Cabal
Cagliostro
Carmilla
Carr
Chan
Chandler
Charteris

Conan
Conan Doyle
Damballa
Dash
Dashiell
Della
Demon
Demon Cat
Dr. Moriarty
Dragon
Dragonwyck
Dürrenmatt
Endore
Evileye
Exorcism
Father Brown
Feer
Freya

James Bond
Jera
Judge Dee
Lasher
Le Carré
Lecter
Lemba
Fu Manchu   Lestat
Ghostory   Ligotti
Gideon Wyck   Lovecraft
Gilles de Rais   Lucifer
Goldfinger   Ludlum
Gormenghast   Maigret
Gothic   Manderley
Groan   Marie Celeste
Hammett   Marlowe
Hoffmann   Mayfair
Holmes   Melchior

Moloch
Moonfleet
Moonstone
Moto
Mycroft
Myst
Nero Wolfe
Nevermore
Ngaio
Pertho
Phantom
Phantasm
Philo
Poirot
Poltergeist
Red Dragon
Rohmer
Rune, Runes

Saint
Sandman
Sarsfield
Sax Rohmer
Sayers
Shadow
Sherlock
Silver Blaze
Stephen King
Stoker
Stonehenge
Sumaru
Tarot
Templar
Thriller
Titus
Tremors
Undine

Vance
Voodoo
Watson
Werecat
Whateley
Wheatley
Whitechapel
Witchcraft
Yeti

NAMES THAT
NO CAT
SHOULD EVER
HAVE

Boxer
Fang
Fido

Gator
Lassie
Rex
Rover
Smokey the
  Cat
Snoop Doggy
  Dog
Snoopy
Spot
Tweetie Bird

ORIENTICATS

Attaturk
Bast
Bastet
Beijing
Bey
Bubastis

Buddha
Butterfly
  Dragon
Byzantium
Chin Ping Mei
Cleocatra
Cleopatra
Confucius
Constanti-
  nople
Dragon
Egg Roll
Genghis
Genji
Hammurabi
Han
Honda
I Ching

Inishiro
Isis
Istanbul
Jasmin
Kaseki
Kobo
Kurosawa
Kyoto
Lao-tze
Mah Jongg
Makioka
Mandala
Ming
Mizoguchi
Muhammed
Omar
Omar
  Khayyam

Osaka
Osiris
Ozu
Pasha
Peking
Ptolemy
Ramses
Ririomin
Rubaiyat
Saladin
Scarab
Scarabus
Sekhmet
Shiatsu
Soong
Soseki
Sultan
Tang

Tanizaki
Tao
Tojo
Torah
Tsing
Waley
Wei
Zarathustra
Zoroaster

PIRATICATS

Armada
Barbary
Barrataria
Benavides
Blackbeard
Booty

Brigand
Buccaneer
Charleston
Corsair
Cove
Dacoit
Damsel
De Soto
Drake
Dubloon
Flibuste
Freebooter
Freeboots
Galleon
Havana
Indies
Kidd
Lafayette

Rackam
Raleigh
Shark
Smuggler
Spanish Main
Sumatra

Lascar
Loot
Madagascar
Morgan
One-Eye
Patchy
Picaroon
Pirate
Plank
Poacher
Privateer

POE CATS

Amontillado
Annabel Lee
Arnheim
Baltimore
Bells
Berenice
C. Auguste
   Dupin
Camelopard

Charmion   Fortunato
Diddling   Helicon
Doctor Tarr   Hop-Frog
Dupin   Israfel
Edgar   Lenore
Eiros   Lespanaye
Eldorado   L'Espanaye
Eleonora   Ligeia
Eulalie   Maelstrom
Eureka   Marie Rogêt
                    Masque
                    Mellonta
                      Tauta

                    Metzenger-
                      stein
                    Minister D.
                    Monos
                    Morella

Mr. Poe
Nevermore
Opium
Pendulum
Poe
Professor
  Fether
Pym
Pym, Gordon
Raven
Sleeper
Sphinx
Tamerlane
Telltale
Thingum Bob
Ulalume
Una
Usher

Valdemar
William
  Wilson
Zante

PUNNY AND
AMUSICATS

Barbaricat
Calcatta
Captain Cool
Catarrh
Catsor
Cat House
Cat-Ebing
Catamite
Catamount
Catbird

Catkin	Conquisticat
Catlin	Crazy Ivan
Catnip	Cream
Catsalot	Democat
Catsanova	Fantasticat
Catsup	Felix
Catandmouse	Franz Katka
Catcall	Halicats
Caterwaul	Havlicat
Catmouse	Hepcat
Catwalk	Heroicat
Cheshire Cat	Historicat
Citizen Cat	Italicat
Cleocatra	Jaws
Cool Cat	Jehosecat
Cool Kitty	Katmandu
Connie	Katsparov
Seleccat	Katzenjammer

Kissy Cat
Kit Carson,
Kitty Carson
Kit Kat
Kitty Cool
Kitty Foyle
Kitty
  O'Rourke
Kitty O'Shea
Lafcatio

Leo
Marquis de
  Cat
Maxicat
Meow
Mercatio
Mexicat
Miss Kitty
Mouse
Mouser
Mouser, Grey
Republicat
Satin Cat
Shadowcat
Sophisticat
Tom Cat
Tom Selleckat
Tweetie

Whiskers

Xcalipurr

Ariel

Banquo

Beatrice

Benedick

Bianca

Bolingbroke

Caliban

Calpurnia

Cordelia

Cymbeline

Dark Lady

Desdemona

Falstaff

Grimalkin

Graymalkin

Guildenstern

Hamlet

Hotspur

Iago

Juliet

Lady Macbeth

Lear

Lysander

Macbeth

Macduff

Malvolio

Mercutio

Miranda

Much Ado

Oberon

Ophelia
Othello
Polonius
Prince Hal
Prospero
Romeo
Rosencrantz
Verona

SOUTHERN
CATS

Alabama
Ashley
Baton Rouge
Beauregard
Biloxi
Calhoun

General Lee
Georgia
Gumtree
Huey
Jackson
Jefferson
    Davis
Johnny Reb
Jubilation T.
    Cornpone
Lester
Lester Mad-
    dox

Louisiana
Magnolia
Memphis
Mississippi
Mobile
Oakey
Orleans
Rhett
Rhett Butler
Savannah
Scarlett
Spanish Moss
St. Augustine
Stonewall
Tarnation
Violet
Virginia

SPORTING CATS

Ali
Babe Ruth
Big O
Bird
Borg
Boris
Bungee
Champ
Coach K.
Cooze
Daily Double
Hondo
Joltin' Joe
Jordan
Magic

Pippen
Rawlings
Red
Say Hey
Spalding
Sweet Lou

Teddy
  Ballgame
The Greatest
Trifecta
Wilson
Wilt

TASTY CATS

Alfredo
Anise
Anisette

Arabica
Basil
Beanie
Burger
Burgundy
Cajun Rice
Cajun
  Popcorn
Cayenne
Chamomile
Champagne
Chardonnay
Chianti

Chili Pepper

Choco

Chocolate

Chop Suey

Cilantro

Cinnamon

Claret

Cobbler

Coffee

Coffee Bean

Creamette

Curry

Darjeeling

Earl Grey

Espresso

Fennel

Frankincense

Fresca

Fumey

Ginger

Green Tea

Herb

Hot Sauce

Hunan

Incense

Jasmine

Java

King Creole

La Choy

Lanson

Lapsang

Lapsang
   Souchong

Latte

Lichee

Lipton

Macaroni
Marinara
Meaty
Mincemeat
Minty
Mocha
Mocha Java

Moët
Mushroom   Patchouli
Myrrh   Peaches
Nutmeg   Peachy
Oolong   Pekoe
Orange Spice   Pepper
Oregano   Pizza Man
Oreo   Primavera
Oysters   Riesling
Oysters   Ronzoni
  Rockefeller   Rose
                  Rosé

Rosemary
Sashimi
Souchong
Spearmint
Spice
Spritzer
Sushi
Sweetmeats
Sweets
Szechuan
Tabasco
Tang
Tangy
Tarragon
Tart
Tasty
Tetley
Thyme

Tokay
Violet
Wintergreen

CATS IN HISTORY

The ancestors of today's cats first evolved about 45 million years ago, during the late Eocene era. By 35 million years ago, ancient cats looked and behaved very much like some members of today's cat family. We're all familiar with the most ferocious ancient cat: the saber-toothed tiger, with its frightening fangs. Though related to the saber-tooth, today's domestic cats descend more directly from another ancestor, an ancient wildcat who was larger than our felines but smaller than lions, tigers, or panthers.

This ancestral wildcat spread slowly around the world, appearing finally in every part of the globe except Australia, Madagascar, Antarctica, the West Indies, and some other islands. By the time the saber-tooth died out about 100,000 years ago, the rest of the cat family had organized itself into the three main groups we still

recognize today. The *Panthera* genus consists of lions, tigers, and other big cats. Cheetahs have a genus all their own, called *Acinonyx,* for cats whose claws do not retract. Small cats make up the genus *Felis*, encompassing pumas, lynxes, and other small wildcats, along with their most familiar descendant, *Felis catus catus*, the domesticated cat with whom we happily share our lives today.

Researchers can track the evolution of cats by their colors. The fur of most ancient cats was probably the shade called "ticked," or *agouti*. Today's wildcats often show this coloration, in which each separate hair is brown or black with a yellow tip. In prehistoric times, a mutation probably caused dark spots to appear in the fur of some cats, giving them a camouflage advantage we still recognize in jungle hunters such as leopards and jaguars. Later, another mutation may have created the stripes we see on today's tabby cats and tigers. White spots appeared last of all. For animals who need the ability to hunt undercover in order to survive, attention-getting patches of white are a major disadvantage. That's why white spots are common today only in domestic cats, who have human help to find food and safety. Cat color offers researchers a way to track the history of domestic cats too. The blotched tabby pattern, for example, first appeared in England. In the United States today, blotched tabby cats are common in areas originally settled by English colonists. But because blotched tabby cats were unusual in sixteenth-century Spain, they're relatively rare now in California, the Southwest, and other areas where the first European settlers were Spanish.

Because cats are loners, they probably found it harder to adjust to domestication than dogs did. Dogs descend from wolves, who are pack animals, used to living as a group and forming strong social bonds. This instinct for close association made it relatively easy for wolves to learn to live with humans, and that's probably why dogs were domesticated thousands of years before cats were. Cats, being cats, they kept to themselves until they found a very good reason to give up their freedom.

The first cats were domesticated 5,000 to 8,000 years ago, in the Nile River Valley in Egypt. Members of the species *Felis sylvestris libyaca,* also known as the African wildcat, were first drawn to domesticity by the human shift from nomadic to agrarian living. Once people learned how to farm, they began to store

their harvested crops. Stored
food attracted rodents, and the
rodents, in turn, attracted wildcats. As the cats demonstrated
their usefulness by controlling
the mouse population, grateful
farmers fed them to encourage
them to stick around.

Liking the food and the
freedom from danger,
the cats chose to stay.
Thus began a long and
mutually beneficial re-
lationship. The ancient
Egyptians named these
cats *miu*, a name that
tells us that, even in ancient times, cats spoke

the same language that our cats do now!

The first domesticated cats weren't just wildcats who chose to allow themselves to be tamed. They differed from other wildcats in one crucial respect: They *enjoyed* human contact. African wildcats are instinctively wary of people, and European wildcats are even more difficult to tame. Wildcats don't learn to snuggle in laps and rub affectionately against their owners' ankles, as domestic cats do.

One researcher tamed and bred some of today's African

wildcats to see if their kittens would become domesticated when raised with people from birth. But the wildcats' kittens never lost their fear of humans. Instead, they cowered when people approached them as fearfully as if they'd been born in the wild. And if humans insisted on handling or controlling them, the kittens turned aggressive, spitting, laying back their ears, and even biting. Another researcher made a similar discovery when he crossed European wildcats with domestic kitties.

The hybrid kittens couldn't be trusted not to hunt and kill ducks and poultry, and if they weren't kept in confinement, they promptly disappeared into the woods.

Researchers think that the affectionate, gentle personality of today's domestic cats began thousands of years ago, with a genetic mutation that made some African wildcats more adaptable to human companionship. Through natural selection, these gentler mutant cats gave rise eventually to today's worldwide legions of purring tabbies, curled up snug in the laps of their very own humans.

The ancient Egyptians worshipped cats in the cult of
Bastet, which began in about
1000 B.C. and lasted until it was
outlawed by Theodosius I in
A.D. 390. Bastet was a goddess
with the head of a cat and the
body of a woman, who repre-
sented fertility and health as
blessings of the Sun. Domestic
cats were sacred to Bastet. At
festivals in her honor, attended
each year by as many as half a
million people, hundreds of
thousands of cats were sacrificed, mummified, and buried.

Mummies examined by today's archeologists show that the sacrificed animals were usually kittens or young cats who died of broken necks. Vast cat cemeteries were located in several Egyptian cities. In 1888, a farmer accidentally dug up one of the cat burial grounds in the Egyptian city of Beni Hasan. Hundreds of thousands of mummified cats were exposed. Children played with them or carried them off to sell to travelers on the Nile, scattering mummy cloth and bits of bones everywhere. Most of the dug-up cat mummies were eventually used for fertilizer. Nineteen tons of mummified cat bones were sent to England to be ground into fertilizer for British farm fields. From that massive shipment, just one skull remains, now preserved in the British Museum.

The ancient Egyptians so honored their cats that the punishment for killing a cat was death. One unfortunate Roman soldier who made the mistake of hurting a cat was torn limb from limb by outraged Egyptians. Even when a cat died naturally, everyone in its home had to don full mourning and shave their eyebrows. While people wailed and lamented, the cat's body would be rolled in a linen sheet and embalmed with drugs and spices.

Rich people's cats were encased in colored linen, which was folded and wound in complicated patterns. A cat-faced mask made of papier-mâché, with ears made of the ribs of palm leaves, was placed over the cat's face, and the resulting mummy was placed in a case made of wood or plaited straw, sometimes decorated with gold, crystal, and obsidian. Even kittens were buried in little bronze coffins.

Poor people's cats got simpler treatment, but they were still buried with honor and ceremony. To feed them in the afterlife, mice and shrews were mummified and put into tombs alongside mummified pets.

The most honored cats were those who served in temples.

Their funerals were sometimes so elaborate and expensive that special taxes were levied to pay for them.

Images of cats begin to appear in Egyptian art starting about 2600 B.C., but the first definite evidence of domestication turned up in a tomb dated about 1900 B.C., in which researchers found the bones of seventeen cats buried with little pots of milk. After about 1600 B.C., cats took on a more prominent role in Egyptian art, curled up under their owners' chairs, chewing on bones, playing with one another, and, in what must be the earliest record of human efforts to confine these independent wanderers, tied to the leg of a chair with a red ribbon. One painting shows the mother of Pharaoh Akhnaton at dinner, slipping bits of food to a kitty under her chair. Another depicts a tabby cat eagerly hunting for birds in the company of a human hunting party.

Egyptian artists painted cats by the hundreds on the walls of tombs and on papyrus. They sculpted cats in bronze, gold, stone, and wood, molded them out of faience, and carved them into ivory. Young Egyptian women used cat amulets, called *utchats*, as fertility tokens, praying to have as many children as the number of kittens shown on the amulet. The word *utchat* spread through the world along with cats themselves, eventually becoming the root for the word *cat* in English, French, Italian, Russian, Hindustani, and many other Indo-European languages.

Cats had been domesticated in Egypt for at least a thousand years before they appeared in the rest of the world. Their spread was slowed by the Egyptians themselves, who revered felines so deeply that, for centuries, they prohibited their export. When Egyptian travelers found domesticated cats living in other countries, they purchased or stole them in order to bring them home to Egypt, where they believed they belonged. Seeing a business opportunity in this Egyptian-imposed feline shortage, the trade-savvy Phoenicians smuggled cats out of Egypt when they could, selling them to wealthy animal lovers in other countries. Thus, domestic cats first appeared along established

Phoenician trade routes, spreading later into the rest of the world. Domestic cats arrived in Greece in 500 B.C., in India about 300 B.C., and in China in 200 B.C. It took longer for cats to make it into Europe. The first domestic cats did not appear in Italy and Switzerland until the first few centuries after the birth of Christ.

The domestic cat changed as it

spread through Europe. Inter-breeding with the European wild-cat, *Felis sylvestris sylvestris*, made European domestic cats stockier and broader than the lean, elegant feline that had first emerged in Egypt. We can still see that difference today by comparing the relatively sturdy European or American shorthair, a breed with plenty of European wildcat genes, to the leaner breeds that evolved in Asia or Africa, such as the graceful Abyssinian or the refined Siamese.

When Herodotus, the Greek traveler, visited Egypt in the

fifth century B.C., he was so intrigued by the cats he saw that he wrote cat-sighting reports in his travel journals. Domestic cats must have arrived in Greece soon thereafter. The first representation of a cat in Greek art appears in a bas-relief from about 500 B.C., showing a cat on a leash facing a dog who is also leashed. As cat and dog eye each other, their owners and a few spectators lean forward, waiting eagerly to see how the animals will respond to one another—an explosive outcome that today's cat and dog owners can predict without pause!

The words the ancient Greeks formed for cats still appear in our language today. *Ailouros*, the Greek name for cat, turns up in our words for someone who loves cats—an *ailurophile*—and for someone who detests or fears them—an *ailurophobe*.

Although the 200,000-year-old

bones of a jungle cat have been found near the Thames River in England, no domestic cats lived in Great Britain until Roman soldiers brought them onto the island. Evidence of cats first begins to appear in British ruins dating from about the fourth century A.D. In Silchester, Hampshire, a cat walked across tiles laid out to dry by an ancient kiln, leaving footprints for archeologists to find fifteen centuries later.

Remains of another cat were found in ruins from the same period in Kent, where a fire destroyed an ancient house and trapped a cat in the basement.

Enough of this cat's body remained for researchers to determine that it was larger than our domesticated cats of today, but smaller than its mummified Egyptian forebears, with a skull that showed the beginnings of the foreshortened nose of today's felines.

By the fifth century in Ireland, a cat was included on a list of goods considered essential for a housewife. And in the ninth century A.D., an illustration of a cat was included in the famous Irish illuminated manuscript, *The Book of Kells*.

The first cats in Great Britain

were revered and respected for their mousing abilities. A cat killer would be severely fined by having to give over a lamb or a sheep, a substantial penalty in those days. In Wales in the tenth century, the legal definition of a hamlet consisted of a place with nine buildings, one herdsman, one plow, one kiln, one churn, one bull, one cock, and one cat. Welsh law established the value of cats. Until its eyes opened, a kitten was worth a penny (the value of a lamb, kid, goose, or hen). When its eyes opened, it was worth two pennies, and once it began to kill mice, its value escalated to four pence. When a husband and wife split up, the husband got to keep a valuable piece of property: the household cat. In the tenth century, one Welsh king punished a cat killer by requiring him to pay the penalty of a pile of grain heaped high enough to cover the cat's body, which had been hung up by its tail so that its nose touched the ground. And in twelfth-century Saxony, anyone who killed a cat had to pay its owner sixty bushels of corn.

In Europe in the Middle Ages,

the early reverence for cats began to shift to suspicion, fear, and finally, outright hatred. Pagans worshipped the Norse goddess Freya, who kept cats around her, used cats to pull her wagon, and was worshipped with cat rituals. As the Christian Church grew, it campaigned against witchcraft and barred the worship of pagan gods and goddesses, including Freya. Friday, the day named after Freya, became known as the Witches' Sabbath, and her cat companions were scorned and feared as witch's familiars.

In the fifteenth century, Pope Innocent VIII ordered all cat worshipers in Europe to be burned as witches, making cat-related witchcraft prosecutions common. In seventeenth-century Denmark, a woman was prosecuted as a witch for allegedly giving birth to a baby with the head of a cat. Doctors today would recognize a tragic birth defect, but to the Danes of that time, the baby's strange features were proof that its mother had consorted with the devil. In 1699, more than 300 children were prosecuted as witches for keeping pet cats. For this offense, fifteen of the children were executed, and others were whipped in front of the church every Sunday for a year. As late as the seventeenth century, Edward Topsell wrote, "The familiars of Witches do most ordinarily appeare in the shape of cats, which is an argument that this beast is dangerous in soule and body."

Historians believe that those who persecuted cats in the Middle Ages may also have punished themselves too. The widespread mistreatment of cats caused the feline population to drop by as much as 90 percent from its previous level. This, in turn, allowed rats to overrun human settlements. As rats increased, so did their fleas, which may have contributed to the spread of the dreaded disease that medieval people called the Black Death.

Today, we know this illness as bubonic plague, and we understand that it is caused by *Yersinia pestis*, a bacterium living on fleas. But medieval Europeans believed that the Black Death was caused by witchcraft, Satan, or poisoned wells. In the fourteenth century, bubonic plague swept through Europe and parts of Asia, killing one-fourth to one-half of the population. Ironically, the cats whose mistreatment may have contributed to the plague epidemic may also have helped to bring it to an end.

While the Black Death raged through Europe, people were too distracted by their own suffering to kill and torment cats. In this climate of relative safety, cat numbers increased. The cats brought the rat population under control, which helped to stem the spread of the plague at last. But those who survived the Black Death failed to show proper gratitude to the cats who had helped them. Instead, many people went right back to killing cats again.

While people in Europe were torturing cats, people in the Middle East and Asia were honoring them. Muslims believed that Mohammed was so fond of his cat that he cut off the sleeve of his robe rather than awaken his cat, who was sleeping on it. As long ago as the thirteenth century, a Muslim sultan directed his heirs to use the earnings from his orchards to care for the stray cats in his neighborhood.

The ancient Chinese kept cats as good-luck omens. Many Chinese people still believe that those who are born in the Year of the Cat have admirable catlike qualities, such as refinement, cleverness, discretion, and high virtue.

In Japan, the first cats arrived in the tenth century. For hundreds of years thereafter, only nobles were allowed to own cats, and the lucky felines were cosseted in every way. At that time, the Japanese name for pet cats was *tama*, which means jewel. All cats in Japan were kept on leashes until 1602, when the gov-

ernment ordered them released,
perhaps to aid in exterminating
rodents who threatened the silk-
worm industry.

Far from being associated with
evil, cats in Japanese folk-
lore often help people or bring
good luck. Tourists today can
visit a cat cemetery in Tokyo
founded centuries ago. The
cemetery's temple facade is decorated by a procession of cats
raising their right forelegs, as if
to bless the felines buried there
in honor.

Some of the first domestic cats to
emerge in Asia probably devel-

oped a genetic mutation that affected their tails. As a result, strange tails have been common in Asian cats throughout history. In 1868, Charles Darwin reported, "Throughout the Malayan Archipelago, Siam, Pegu, and Burmah, all the cats have truncated tails about half the proper length, often with a sort of knot at the end." Ascribing tail problems to all Asian cats may have been an exaggeration. But in 1959, a cat researcher named A. G. Searle confirmed Darwin's observation in part, noting that about one-third of the cats in Hong Kong, and two-thirds of those in Malaysia, had kinks in their tails.

The prevalence of tail oddities in Asian cats led scientists to conclude that the Manx cat, first noticed in England, must have arrived there on ships originating in Asia. Some Manx, called "rumpies," have no tails at all, while "stumpies" have only partial tails.

Siamese cats, who also originated in Asia, often have kinks in their tails. An old legend explains that the purpose of this kink was to allow princesses to keep their rings safe while bathing. The royal ladies were said to hang their jewelry on the tails of their Siamese cats, where the kinks kept the valuables securely in place. A more scientific explanation holds that the kink is an inherited abnormality of the caudal vertebrae, caused by the same genetic mutation that altered the tails of many other Asian cats.

By the seventeenth and eighteenth centuries, European hostility toward cats was beginning to subside. Slowly, cats began to take their places once more as valued pets. In mid-seventeenth-century France,

Cardinal Richelieu kept dozens of them at court, and when he died, he provided for the care of his kitties in his will.

As the eighteenth century began, European princesses and fashionable French court ladies pampered their pet cats, holding salons to discuss their virtues, engraving their images on medals, and burying them in lavish tombs. French artists like Watteau and Fragonard included cats in paintings of pastoral outdoor scenes, as well as in pictures of ladies' boudoirs. One French astronomer, Lalande, even added a new constellation in the shape of a cat, called *Felis*, to eighteenth-century star charts.

In England, too, domesticated cats began to reappear in stories, poems, and pictures of happy family life. The painter Stubbs even celebrated a friendship between a horse and a cat when he included a black stable cat in his portrait of the famous racehorse, Godolphin. By the nineteenth century, Queen Victoria's cat, White Heather, was so popular that she had her own biography. Soon thereafter, the first societies for the prevention of animal cruelty were established, in part to make sure that the cruel treatment meted out to cats and other animals during the Middle Ages would never be socially acceptable again.

As the Industrial Revolution virtually transformed nineteenth-century England, almost everyone went to work in factories, offices, and warehouses—including cats, who controlled rodents for many burgeoning new businesses. In the British Post Office, the rodent-control contributions of cats were so valued that in 1868, a Cat System was inaugurated to provide for the comfort and upkeep of all the Post Office cats.

Muriel Beadle, author of *The Cat: History, Biology and Behavior*, writes that under the system, the secretary of the Post Office financed the purchase of cat food by providing each branch office with six or seven pence per cat. But to make sure the feline employees didn't get so comfortable that they forgot their jobs, the secretary never provided quite enough money. He directed that the cats "must depend on the mice for the remainder of their emoluments." In the tradition of bureaucrats everywhere, branch managers appealed regularly for higher cat budgetary allotments.

In 1873, one postmaster succeeded when he explained that he needed extra money not just for the cost of cat food, but also to make up for "the loss of dignity when carrying the cat's food through the streets in Her Majesty's uniform." The Post Office cats proved to be so helpful in controlling Post Office mice that official cats still prowled British post offices in the 1970s, more than a century after the Cat System first began.

Throughout history, animals have helped people. Cows give milk,

sheep give wool, horses provide transportation—and cats prove their value to humanity by hunting. In the late fifteenth century, Conquistador Diego de Almagro paid 600 pieces of eight for the first domestic cat in South America, imported to control mice. Frederick the Great, king of Prussia in the eighteenth century, ordered every town he conquered to pay a levy of cats, who kept rodents out of his army's stores.

Centuries later, cats came to the rescue one more time as part of the Marshall Plan, executed by the United States to help rebuild Europe after World War II. To feed starving people, Americans shipped hundreds of thousands of tons of grain into Europe. Borrowing a time-honored technique from the ancient Egyptians, they sent 10,000 cats along with the grain to keep it safe from mice. The cats did their part, helping to keep the grain intact so that hungry Europeans could restore their strength and begin the long process of rebuilding the war-shattered continent.

In 1964, an epidemic of Bolivian hemorrhagic fever swept through San Joaquin, a remote settlement in the Andes, caused by wild mice who carried the Machupo virus. After a radio appeal for help, hundreds of donated cats were airlifted to the stricken community, bringing the epidemic to a halt.

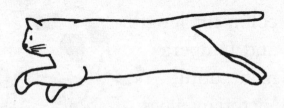

The basic body structure and appearance of the cat has changed surprisingly little through history. People created dog breeds on purpose, selecting traits like size, aggressiveness, or speed that suited dogs for particular tasks. But most cat breeds arose accidentally, as a result of genetic isolation in far-flung parts of the world. People did not begin to notice or value the different cat breeds, with their fascinating variety in color, fur length, and temperament, until Victorian times, when travelers began to bring home some of the odd-looking cats they encountered in exotic spots.

The shorthaired cats are the oldest European breed, descending from the first cats distributed through Europe by the Romans. Manx cats first came from Asia, the Angora from Turkey, the Persian from Asia Minor, the Siamese from the Far East, and the Abyssinian from Ethiopia. As breeds like these acquired names and popularity, cat owners began to want to show them off to one another.

The first cat show was held at

the Crystal Palace in London in 1871. In Europe and North America today, more than 100 different pedigree breeds have been officially established with standards and registries. But for all their remarkable differences, cats from the various breeds are all variations on one theme: the astonishingly beautiful, complex, and well-loved domestic cat.

CATS IN LITERATURE

It is a little-known fact that James Joyce, the Irish writer best known for his *Dubliners* stories and the epic *Ulysses*, once wrote a fable. What began as a letter to his grandson Stephen in 1936 became the children's story, "The Cat and the Devil." It is the tale of a certain bridge

over the River Loire in France
that the devil himself promises
to build for the people of
Beaugency. In exchange for his
good deed, he wants for himself
the first person who crosses the
bridge. The mayor of the town

agrees to the deal, but tricks the devil by sending over a black cat instead of a person. This angers the devil, who from then on calls the townspeople *les chats de Beaugency*, the "cat people." He sympathizes, however, with the poor cat who crossed the bridge and has jumped into his arms. He takes him as his own, and the two (as we know from history) become lifelong companions.

It's not surprising that writer Edgar Allan Poe would pen a spooky short story about a witchy black cat. In his story appropriately titled "The Black Cat," the main character is a man quite fond of animals, including his large black cat, Pluto. As bad luck would have it, the man becomes annoyed with his furry friend, then angry, and finally foul-tempered and abusive, and cuts out the cat's eye. Faithful Pluto forgives him, which upsets the man even more, enough so that he hangs the cat from a tree.

One evening, another cat, black with white markings on his chest (and also missing an eye), follows him home. The two become companions, but in time, the man, in a rage of psychosis, tries to kill the cat with an ax. Luckily for the cat, the man's wife interrupts the scene, only to get the ax buried deep in her head. The man hides her body in a wall, but his hideous act is given away when the cat, who had mistakenly been buried in the wall, too, cries out and is heard by the police. The pattern of the white fur on the black cat's chest now reveals . . . the gallows!

We all know that most cats are good at mousing and taking naps, but they're also pretty good writers. In 1942, Christopher Cat, in collaboration with Countee Cullen, a leading poet of the Negro Renaissance of the 1920s, wrote a book. *My Lives and How I Lost Them* is the cat's account of his nine lives and what fates he met along the way, including drowning and getting caught in a rat trap. It is a humorous, sophisticated piece of writing by one very intelligent cat that was certainly ahead of his time!

What's it like to be a Shakespearean actor and have to learn how to use a litter box? Win-stanley Fortescue, the protagonist in mystery novelist Marian Babson's *Nine Lives to Murder*, can tell you. Babson, who dedicates her book to "all the cats in our lives, and the life in our cats," adds comic fantasy to this story of an actor being pursued by a murderer. Before the evildoer has his chance, Fortescue falls unconscious and lands on the acting company's cat, Montmorency D. Mousa. When Fortescue comes to, his body has been switched with the cat's. What transpires is a tale of feline experiences that make you glad you don't have to eat mice for dinner!

The cat has always been an animal of mystery, so it follows that cats feel right at home in mystery stories. Writer Lilian Jackson Braun features cats as detectives in her mystery novel series that includes *The Cat Who Said Cheese* and *The Cat Who Blew the Whistle*. Journalist Jim Qwilleran and his feline sleuths Koko and Yum Yum wander Pickax City trying to solve mysterious bombings, murders, missing persons, and the like. These books are as tantalizing as catnip and will have readers wishing these cats prowled *their* neighborhoods at night.

Sneaky Pie Brown is yet another cat author who, together with screenwriter and poet Rita Mae Brown, pens the "Mrs. Murphy" mystery series. Sneaky Pie's main characters are Mary Minor Haristeen and her clever cat, Mrs. Murphy. Together, these two solve crimes, sometimes with the help of a Welsh corgi and a fat, gray cat, in novels like *Wish You Were Here, Rest in Pieces,* and *Murder at Monticello.* Mrs. Murphy's experiences with her circle of animal friends and insights into human emotions provide the reader with a cat's perspective on life. Still don't believe cats can write? Sneaky Pie Brown's pawprint in the "Author's Note" proves it.

The cat in Rudyard Kipling's "The Cat That Walked by Himself" is the embodiment of the typically independent nature of the truly curious cat. The story describes a time when animals were wild and Man and Woman lived in caves. Cat is determined not to lose his independence as

Dog, Cow, and Horse did when they became tamed by humans; he declares he will always walk alone and go wherever, whenever, he pleases. He makes the following bargain with Woman: If Cat ever overhears Woman praising him, she will let him into the cave, where he can sit by the fire and drink milk. One day, Cat stops Woman's baby from crying and entertains him by chasing a string. Woman compliments Cat and, thereby, fulfills the bargain. Cat can enter the cave, get warm, and eat at his leisure, but he is still untamed and free to come and go as he wishes. Unfortunately, Dog makes his own bargain with Cat and chases him up a tree whenever he gets the opportunity! Such is the life of a cat.

Tom Quartz, a name later used by Theodore Roosevelt for one of his own kittens, is a miner's feline companion in Mark Twain's short story, "Dick Baker's Cat." Baker tells his fellow mining friends the story of when Tom Quartz, who cared little for hunting rats but had a keen ability to find gold, almost meets his doom in the blasting of a quartz mine. He survives the explosion with singed whiskers and remains as smug (if not a little intimidating, as cats can be!) as ever.

Who is not familiar with Dr. Seuss's fun-loving Cat in the Hat in his zany striped hat? Perhaps the best-known cat in contemporary children's literature, the energetic cat who waltzes into the home of two bored children on a rainy day is known to inspire young and old to learn how to read. Quite an undertaking for such a silly rhyming puss! Dr. Seuss used only 220 words for this classic, yet it remains a timeless favorite of children and parents all over the globe. If you don't remember what mischievous tricks this cat has under his hat, perhaps you should reacquaint yourself— you'll be glad you did!

Do you remember the three little kittens who lost their mittens? They cried because they could have no pie. They then found their mittens and cried again until their mother gave them the pie. As naughty kittens will do, they soiled their mittens and then had to wash them. What happens at the end of this childhood rhyme? Their mother smells a rat! This somewhat nonsensical poem has pleased generations of kiddies—not to mention *kitties!*

"I've often seen a cat without a grin, but a grin without a cat?" The most famous cat in all of British children's literature is probably the one Alice meets in Lewis Carroll's *Through the Looking Glass*. With a wide, toothy grin, the Cheshire Cat sits in the bough of a tree and looks down at poor Alice, who is lost. When the girl asks him what direction she should take, he, a cat of quick wit, says: "That depends a good deal on where you want to get to." Perhaps more intriguing than his intelligence is the Cheshire Cat's ability to disappear, a little bit at a time, a quality that helps him escape execution by the king.

Did you know that it may have been a mouse who invented the belled cat collar? Aesop writes about mice that fear a cat in his fable, "The Bell and the Cat." The mice are hungry, beginning to starve, in fact, but a cat looms outside their hole, and so they are afraid to go in search of crumbs. A bold mouse makes the suggestion that they tie a bell around the cat's neck so they'll know when the cat is near. Good idea, the mice think, but one elder mouse rises and asks the all-important question: "Who will bell the cat?"

Puss in Boots, the matchmaker cat who wears red boots in the old French children's story, is the type of cat everyone wants: He's clever, charming, and a good hunter. Puss knows his master is poor, so he places himself in favor with the king and devises a way for the man to meet with the beautiful royal daughter. His plan works, and his master becomes rich when he marries the princess. What becomes of Puss? He becomes a lord, of course!

The cat that accompanies an explorer on a 1914 expedition to Antarctica must be one *cool* cat! *Mrs. Chippy's Last Expedition: The Remarkable Journal of Shackleton's Polar-Bound Cat* by Caroline Alexander (with an introduction by Lord Mouser-

Hunt F.R.G.S.), a book you just might mistake for a real-life story, is the heroic tale of Mrs. Chippy, a tiger-striped tabby. He is an optimistic and physically fit male cat (despite the Mrs. in his name) who survives the shipwreck of *Endurance*, a vessel headed into icy waters. The detailed journal of his life on the ship is complemented by black-and-white photography of him and his shipmates.

American horror writer H. P. Lovecraft had a great affection for cats and often included them in his short stories. "Something

About Cats" is an essay on the majestic and highly intelligent qualities of the cat in comparison to the "slavering devotion and obedience" of dogs. According to his wife, Lovecraft, who enjoyed walking the streets of New York City alone in the darkness of night, seemed to speak a language that cats understood. Pet cats doted on him, even when he was not their owner. It seems he was inspired by the mysterious and aloof animal, if not somehow more closely related to them.

William Shakespeare himself

scattered cats through-
out his great works. A
tawny cat sits with
the three witches
at the start of *Macbeth*. One
witch is even named "Graymalkin," an ancient cat name.
As the three hags sit in their
cave preparing evil spells
against the king, their cat friend
gives the signal ("thrice the
brinded cat hath mewed") to
begin their witchy session.

If you think cats and mice can
never put aside their differences
long enough to become friends,
read George Selden's children's

book, *The Cricket in Times Square*. Tucker, a mouse who lives in a New York City subway drainpipe, becomes friends and shares his home with a roving cat named Harry, a fugitive from the East Side. The unusual friendship between cat and mouse is explained by way of the unconventional attitudes characteristic of the Big Apple. "In

New York, we gave up these old habits long ago," says Harry.

A. A. Milne's Tigger may not be domesticated, but he's probably as close as he can get. The beloved, energetic tiger in the Winnie the Pooh stories is clearly not a typical feline. Instead of slinking around with intimidating slyness, Tigger just bounces until he can bounce no more. He is rather optimistic, in contrast to the smug, sometimes sarcastic attitude of many cats in literature. Tigger *is* a cat's cat, however; he likes to do as he pleases, where he pleases . . . and he *doesn't* like honey!

In "How the Cat Became," a story by Ted Hughes, Cat is a lazy animal who just wants to sleep in the sun all day and play his violin at night. The other animals, who think he's strange and unlike any of them, urge him to get a job. Cat likes his life of leisure, but the others' proddings make him get up one day and go ask Man for employment on his farm. Cat becomes the rat and mouse catcher, but makes sure he only catches enough so he won't ever run out of rodents and lose his job. This way, he can lounge in the fields all day and make music at night as soon as he has collected a satisfactory pile of critters for Man.

Edgar Allan Poe wasn't the only person to write a short story called "The Black Cat." William Wintle, a British writer, wrote a story of the same title about Sydney, a wealthy man of leisure who dislikes and fears cats, but at the same time is entranced by the curious creatures. As time passes, he becomes obsessed with the animal, thinking he sees black cats in heaps of dirt and museum antiques. He is visited one night by a large, black cat that has appeared to him in a nightmare, the same cat who begins to follow him like a shadow. Sydney is eventually torn to pieces by the bad kitty, who seems to sense the man's hatred of felines.

"Venus and the Cat," one of Aesop's more famous fables, is about a cat who falls in love with a man. The cat begs the goddess Venus to change her into a woman so that the man might love her back. Venus obliges and the two young lovers marry. One day, Venus decides to see if the young woman has given up her "catty"

instincts and lets a mouse loose in the girl's bedroom. The girl pounces on the mouse to the disgust of Venus, who promptly changes her back into a cat! The moral of the story: One can change one's appearance but not one's nature.

In the Chinese tale "Why the Dog and the Cat Are Enemies,"

there lives a poor couple with a cat and a dog. One day, the dog has the brilliant idea of obtaining a gold ring that will make the couple rich and happy. The cat agrees to help the dog carry out the scheme. The cat is faster than the dog and returns to their masters with the ring, leaving the dog far behind. The cat is praised for being so quick and smart while the dog is beaten for being slow and unhelpful. The cat says nothing, so the angry dog, having been cheated of any reward, chases and bites her. The story explains why cats and dogs don't get along to this day.

Quentin Patrick's 1945 short story "The Fat Cat" once again proves the nine lives theory of tabbies. The fat cat, who remains nameless, has befriended an American corporal in World War II Japan. Knowing the cat will be killed if it follows him into enemy territory, the corporal stops feeding it in hopes it might seek out someone else's company. The cat is devoted, however, and follows the corporal through miles of jungle to a recently deserted enemy camp. There the famished soldier finds a table of food, including a roast chicken, which the cat sees too and starts to eat. The corporal throws a rock at the cat to chase him away but instead hits the chicken, which explodes because it has been booby-trapped. Had the corporal touched the chicken, he would have been killed. So, in an odd and unexpected way, the fat cat—who survives the blast—saves the man's life.

In P. G. Wodehouse's *The Story of Webster*, Lancelot is a free-spirited artist. But once he adopts Webster the cat, he becomes intimidated and insecure whenever his new pet even glances at him. Lancelot changes his behavior to try to please Webster and hopes that just once he will catch the cat in a weak moment. Of course, he does; he finds Webster lapping up some spilled rum and getting downright intoxicated! The man's self-consciousness disappears and he returns to living his life as he pleases. Webster, after all, is just "one of the boys."

Tom is naughty, and so are his sisters. In Beatrix Potter's "Tom Kitten," part of her *Tales of Peter Rabbit*, Tom, Mittens, and Moppet get dressed up by their mother and are told to wait in the garden for her guest to arrive for afternoon tea. Instead, the bad kittens climb a stone wall, get dirty, and even lose their nice clothes to the puddle-ducks. Needless to say, they are punished when they return home—but that doesn't stop them from climbing the curtains and having still more fun in their bed-room!

Have you ever looked outside at night to see the neighborhood cat staring up into the sky? M. Grant Cormack's story, "Why the Cat Stares at the Moon" offers a perfectly good explanation for pussy's strange behavior. It seems that once upon a time, Dog played a trick on Cat to protect Mouse. Cat was always after Mouse, so Dog told Cat that his tiny, gray prey had gone to visit the Man in the Moon. When Cat sits looking up at the Moon, he is waiting for Mouse

to return on a moonbeam. Silly
old Cat!

Legend has it that a particular
cat used to work grinding coffee
in the king's kitchen. One day,
this cat decides to watch the
king's regal procession into the
city; he swallows the coffee mill
and blames thieves for stealing
it before sneaking out. When he
returns, a low, grinding noise
comes from his throat as the

king pats him. Realizing that the noise comes from the mill in the cat's stomach, the king curses all cats. According to *How Cats Came to Purr*, by John Bennett, when a human strokes a cat, the purring heard is a reminder of the cat's ancestor's guilt and shame. And you thought it was a sign of contentment!

Not all cats are as ungrateful as literature might lead one to believe. Take the white cat in Agnes A. Sandham's story, "The Conscientious Cat." She lives with gold miners in the Sierra Nevadas. As thanks for being adopted and cared for, she takes upon herself the duty of warning the men whenever she feels a wall of the mine beginning to crumble. She earns the reputation of a true feline heroine, while the miners' dog sits in a corner with his tail between his legs, ashamed of his laziness.

CELLULOID CATS

PEPPER, THE FELINE SUPERSTAR OF SILENT FILMS

From silent films to the latest box-office blockbuster, cats have captivated viewers on the silver screen.

In fact, the first feline superstar appeared in movies long before "talkies" were invented.

According to the book *Hollywood Cats* by J. C. Suares, Pepper the cat was an audience favorite throughout the silent movie era of the 1920s.

And she became a star without even having to audition!

Legend has it that famed Keystone Cops director Mack Sennett was shooting a movie at his studio in Hollywood when a gray cat snuck in through a broken floorboard. She was included in the scene that was being shot, performed like a natural, and Sennett, who named her Pepper, put her into many of his silent films.

Because of her natural curiosity, Pepper learned fast. For instance, she convincingly played checkers in a scene with comedian Ben Turpin.

However, Pepper's creative career came to an unusual close. The cat had become close buddies with Teddy, a Great Dane who was also in many of Sennett's movies. When Teddy died, Pepper actually went into mourning for her dear, departed partner and retired from movie making.

ORANGEY, THE FELINE SUPERSTAR OF THE FIFTIES, PART I

One of the most talented cats in the history of the motion pictures was Orangey, a large, ginger tabby who starred in the 1951 film *Rhubarb* as well as many other movies. Orangey's film career lasted from the early 1950s through 1963, and during that time, he won more awards than any other cat in Tinseltown.

A shorthaired, photogenic, fluffy (some would say overweight), fourteen-pound feline, Orangey—for all his movie-star glamour—was short-tempered, hard to work with, and nasty. The cat was disliked even by his trainer, Frank Inn! Orangey's antics were so aggravating that a movie executive actually called him "The World's Meanest Cat," and during one film shoot, guard dogs were even placed at the doors of the movie studio to keep Orangey from running away.

But Orangey could act!

He was considered by many to be one of the best animal actors in the world, and he is the only cat to have won the Patsy Award twice, an honor given for best performance by an animal in a movie.

Orangey won the award for his title role in *Rhubarb*, a movie about a cat who inherits a fortune and then buys the Brooklyn Dodgers baseball team. Based on a novel of the same name by H. Allen Smith, Orangey's costars in this big-screen adventure were Ray Milland, Jan Sterling, Leonard Nimoy, and Gene Lockhart.

During the shooting of this movie, Orangey was kept on a leash so that he wouldn't bolt from the set. Even so, he managed to harass everyone around him—including his four-legged stand-ins!

ORANGEY, THE FELINE SUPERSTAR OF THE FIFTIES, PART II

Orangey won another Patsy Award for his memorable performance as the appropriately named character Cat in *Breakfast at Tiffany's*, which starred Audrey Hepburn as Holly Golightly, and also featured a first-class cast, including George Peppard, Buddy Ebsen, Mickey Rooney, and Patricia Neal.

In the film, which is based on a Truman Capote novella, Cat is Holly's beloved pet, whom she calls "a poor slob without a name." During his performance,

Orangey had to jump on Hepburn's back while she lay in bed, leap off Peppard's shoulders onto a shelf, and look quite pathetic as he gets drenched in a rainstorm scene. This scene occurs at the end of the movie when Holly throws Cat out onto the streets of New York City to show that she is a free spirit and not attached to anyone—or anything. Minutes later, she has a change of heart and runs through the pouring rain to find Cat, which, happily, she does!

Orangey's other major film roles include an appearance with Jackie Gleason in *Gigot,* and he was also seen on a regular basis on the famed *Our Miss Brooks* television series, starring Eve Arden and Gale Gordon.

Movie critics and animal trainers agree that, in many of his movies, Orangey often stole the show from his famous costars. If there ever was a feline superstar who should have his pawprints in cement, it was this talented, irascible cat!

THAT DARN CAT, THE ORIGINAL VERSION

When Walt Disney Productions made the movie *That Darn Cat*

in 1965, a Siamese named Syn Cat played the title role of D.C., short for Darn Cat.

In the film, D.C. is a feline that finds a watch belonging to a woman who had been taken hostage during a bank robbery. D.C. brings the watch to her owner, played in the film by a teenage Hayley Mills, and this attracts the attention of an FBI agent. He, of course, finds it difficult to be around cats, yet he follows D.C. through many adventures to crack the case.

"Walt Disney came down to the set when we'd be working with the cat, because he was very interested in how the trainer would get the cat to do certain things," said Dean Jones, who played the FBI agent in the film. "We learned then that cats don't work for love. Cats work for *food*. They're *very* smart."

That Darn Cat was a big hit at the box office and won Syn Cat a Patsy Award. The superb Siamese also received raves from critics, including the *New York Times*, calling the cat's performance one of "suavity and grace." The movie was based on the book *Undercover Cat*, written by Gordon and Mildred Gordon, and it featured quite a famous supporting cast, including Roddy Mc-Dowall, Elsa Lanchester, Ed Wynn, Frank Gorshin, and Dorothy Provine.

That Darn Cat was remade in 1997 as a film that again featured Dean Jones.

THAT DARN CAT, THE REMAKE

That Darn Cat was remade in 1997 by Walt Disney Productions. It starred Christina Ricci as the teenage owner of a cat that finds a clue to a mysterious kidnapping, and Doug E. Doug as the novice FBI agent who follows the cat to solve the case.

As in the original 1965 film, the cat is again named D.C. In this version, however, D.C. is played by a gray-and-white tabby named Elvis, who was found and trained by Larry Madrid.

"I stopped by the North Hollywood animal shelter on my way to the airport for a film assignment and found him there," Madrid said. "I called one of our trainers and said, 'You have to come and get this cat. It's a perfect double for our other cats.' And he ended up being the star of the picture!

"You can tell just by looking at

Elvis. His attitude, his demeanor, the way he carries himself, the looks that he gives you—he acts like a star, and he *is* a star. And he did a great job," the trainer said.

According to the film's production notes, Elvis spends his spare time playing at his scratching post, running around, and hunting. His favorite food is chicken.

"Cats are not the hardest animals to train," Madrid said. "However, people don't expect as much out of them as they do a dog, for example. We teach them to come to a mark and then they are rewarded with food."

The remake of *That Darn Cat* also features a well-known supporting cast, including Academy Award–winner Estelle Parsons, Dyan Cannon, and Dean Jones, who also appeared in the first version of this classic cat comedy.

CATS IN DRAMATIC FILMS, PART I

Numerous poignant films have been created featuring cats on journeys to find their owners.

The Incredible Journey, made in 1963, tells the story of a Siamese cat who joins up with a Labrador retriever and a bull terrier to find the owner they mistakenly believe has left them forever. They embark on a 250-mile trek across Canada's rugged terrain and have many adventures as they search to find their human. This live-action Walt Disney movie was based on Sheila

Burnford's noted book, and it tells the tale from the animal's point of view.

Homeward Bound: The Incredible Journey is a 1993 remake by Walt Disney Productions of the original *The Incredible Journey.* However, this time the animals have voices, supplied by stars Sally Field, Michael J. Fox, and Don Ameche.

The Adventures of Milo & Otis, made in 1989, tells the delightful story of a trouble-prone kitten named Milo who is carried away by a rushing river, and Otis, a pug-nosed pup who sets out to save his friend. The two have many adventures, which are narrated by Dudley Moore, who also supplies all of the voices for the animals in this live-action movie made by Japanese director Masanori Hata. It was a record-breaking box-office success in his homeland.

CATS IN DRAMATIC FILMS, PART II

In the memorable 1974 movie *Harry & Tonto*, Art Carney plays an old man who travels across the country with his cat, Tonto. The film was a huge success for Carney, who won an

Academy Award for his role, as well as for Tonto, who won a Patsy Award for his part in the film as a large, aging cat who has his own leash and suitcase, purrs whenever he is scolded, and is a compassionate companion until he sadly passes away.

There is some sadness in the 1963 movie, *The Three Lives of Thomasina,* in which a little girl's pet cat, Thomasina, is diagnosed with tetanus and is put to sleep. However, in this Walt Disney fairy tale, which takes place in Scotland at the turn of the century, a mysterious healer brings the animal back to life and into the arms of the girl who had mourned her.

In the unusual French film, *Le Chat (The Cat)*, Academy Award–winning actress Simone Signoret and Jean Gabin play a long-married couple who fall out of love. The husband then transfers his affections to his pet cat, with upsetting results to the marital relationship. The movie is based on a novel by famous author Georges Simenon.

CATS IN MYSTERY MOVIES, PART I: THE BLACK CAT

Black cats have been symbols of mystery, mayhem, and even murder in motion pictures.

One of the first famous horror films featuring felines is *The Black Cat*. Made in 1934, it featured a nameless black cat who starred with Bela Lugosi and Boris Karloff in their first movie together. *The Black Cat* was very loosely based 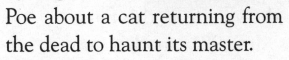 on the famous terrifying tale by Edgar Allan Poe about a cat returning from the dead to haunt its master.

This film is still highly regarded. It has become a cult favorite because of its unusual surreal design, its pairing of Karloff and Lugosi, and because it is one of the very few films in which horror star Lugosi actually plays a good guy!

Universal Studios made another version of *The Black Cat* in 1941 that also starred Bela

Lugosi. In this adaptation of the Poe story, the film is about a woman who keeps a creepy crematorium for her adored feline pets. As it turns out, the cats are the villains in this film.

In 1981 another movie version of *The Black Cat* was made as a low-budget exploitation horror flick in Italy. The movie was so graphic, it actually garnered an "R" rating.

CATS IN MYSTERY MOVIES, PART II: CAT PEOPLE

Perhaps the most famous horror film featuring felines is *Cat*

People, made in 1942 and starring Simone Simon and Kent Smith.

The movie is about a timid woman, played by Simon, who believes that she is carrying the curse of the panther with her. In one scene, Simon's character is given a kitten by her boyfriend, and the kitten hisses in terror when it is placed in her arms. In the film, this is the first clue that Simon's character has a troubled relationship with the world of cats.

Cat People is a very highly regarded film today, in part because the director, Jacques Tourneur, left much of the horror to the audience's imagination rather than showing it explicitly.

The same cannot be said for the 1982 remake of this scary classic. Also titled *Cat People*, the movie stars Nastassja Kinski and Malcolm McDowell, and it includes profanity, nudity, and over-the-top gore.

CATS IN MYSTERY MOVIES: PART III

Cats have appeared in many other suspense flicks, mystery movies, and horror films of varying quality over the years. There

is something about the mysteriousness of felines that attracts the attention of filmmakers—and audiences—all over the world.

These feline flicks include the 1946 horror movie, *The Cat Creeps*, which most critics considered a true horror. It tells the grisly tale of a cat who possesses a young girl's soul.

In the 1961 shocker *The Shadow of the Cat*, a cat seeks revenge for the murder of its owner.

In the 1969 thriller *Eye of the Cat*, Michael Sarrazin and Eleanor Parker star in the creepy story of a woman living in a house full of very frightening felines.

The 1973 television movie *The Cat Creature* stars Meredith Baxter and Oscar winner Gale Sondergaard in the terrifying tale of a cat goddess who possesses her victims to get a gold amulet.

And *Cat's Eye* is a star-studded 1985 thriller, based on a trio of stories written by best-selling horror author Stephen King. Featuring James Woods, Drew Barrymore, Alan King, and many others, this film stars a silver tabby who, as a stray, wanders through each of the three tales. This cat was trained by Karl Lewis Miller and Teresa Ann Miller, and many critics seemed to feel that the feline outperformed many of his costars.

CATS IN SCIENCE
FICTION FILMS

In the 1957 famous science-fiction hit, *The Incredible Shrinking Man,* Grant Williams plays a man who is exposed to a radioactive mist and begins to become smaller—and smaller. As a two-inch-high man, Williams is hunted by a mean-spirited house cat who, of course, is huge in comparison to him. Special effects, including the use of a giant paw, were used to show Williams fighting off the cat in this sci-fi film.

There were felines in outer

space—literally—in the aptly named 1978 Walt Disney movie, *The Cat from Outer Space*. This film tells the story of a cat who comes from beyond the stars and wears a magical collar. The cat needs help from the United States to repair its spaceship and return to its native planet, but gets involved with civilians, spies, and the military before blasting off to a happy ending. The film stars Ken Berry, Sandy Duncan, Harry

Morgan, Roddy McDowall, and Amber the cat, who won a Patsy Award for her performance.

A year later, in 1979's super-successful sci-fi film *Alien*, Sigourney Weaver, who plays Officer Ripley on the spaceship *Nostromo*, is planning her escape from the alien creature who has taken over the spacecraft. However, when she can't find her cat, Jones, Ripley panics and won't leave until she finds him—which she does.

Of course, the character Catwoman, of the hit *Batman* television series and motion pictures, always had many cats surrounding her. Whether Catwoman was played by Julie Newmar, Lee Meriwether, or Eartha Kitt on television, or by Michelle Pfeiffer on the big screen, she was rarely seen in her lair without dozens and dozens of her feline friends surrounding her.

FELINE MOVIE MUSICALS

Ever since a real-life Gene Kelly danced with the animated Tom and Jerry cat and mouse characters in the 1945 musical *Anchors Aweigh*, felines have been featured in movie musicals.

For instance, in 1962, no less

a composer than the esteemed Harold Arlen of *Wizard of Oz* fame provided the music for the full-length animated musical, *Gay Purr-ee*. The movie featured an all-star cast of voices, including those of Judy Garland, Robert Goulet, Red Buttons, Hermione Gingold, and Mel Blanc.

This feature film told the story of a country cat named Mewsette, who goes to Paris looking for love and adventure. After winding up in the paws of a scoundrel cat named Meowrice, she is rescued by her tomcat boyfriend from home.

In 1997, another full-length animated musical featuring felines titled *Cats Don't Dance* was created. In this major movie, a song-and-dance cat named Danny goes from Kokomo, Indiana, to Hollywood seeking fame and fortune; however, his career dreams get threatened by a ruthless child actress.

Complete with original songs

written by Randy Newman, dance legend Gene Kelly was a consultant on the choreography sequences for this lively film, which features voices provided by Natalie Cole, Scott Bakula, Jasmine Guy, Hal Holbrook, Don Knotts, and George Kennedy.

FELINE WINNERS OF THE PATSY AWARD, PART I

For almost four decades, the Patsy Awards were given out by the American Humane Association to honor the top performing animal in television and motion pictures. This award also recognized strict compliance with high humane standards in films that featured animals.

Awards were given to animals in four different categories: canine, equine, wild animals, and "special," a category that included cats. The Patsy Awards were established in 1951 and discontinued in 1989, but in those years, cats won numerous honors for their performances in film and on television.

Some of the following Patsy Award winners were actually considered accomplished actors by their peers, and others acted every inch the Hollywood star!

FELINE WINNERS OF THE PATSY AWARD, PART II

The feline winners of the Patsy Award include:

1952   Orangey, *Rhubarb* (Paramount Pictures); Motion Pictures, First Place

1959   Pyewacket, *Bell, Book, and Candle* (Columbia Pictures); Motion Pictures, First Place. Pyewacket was a Siamese cat who played a big part in this film costarring Kim Novak as a witch who tries to win James Stewart's love.

1962   Orangey, *Breakfast at*

Tiffany's (Paramount
Pictures); Motion Pictures,
First Place
1966   Syn Cat, *That Darn Cat*
(Walt Disney Productions);
Motion Pictures, First Place
1973   Morris, 9-Lives cat
food; Special Commercial
Award, First Place
1974-Midnight, *Mannix*
(Paramount); Television
Series, First Place
1975   Tonto, *Harry and Tonto*
(Twentieth Century–Fox
Studios); Motion Pictures,
First Place
1977   Seventeen, *Dr. Shrinker*
(Sid and Marty Krofft);

Special Category, First Place
1978   Amber, *The Cat from Outer Space* (Walt Disney Productions); Special Category, First Place
1986   The Cats, *Alfred Hitchcock Presents* (Universal Studios); Special Category, First Place

CATS IN ANIMATED FILMS AND TELEVISION, PART I: TOM AND JERRY

Many of the most famous cats in movies have been of the animated variety.

For instance, the cat-and-mouse duo of Tom and Jerry has been delighting movie audiences since 1940, when they appeared in the MGM short, *Puss Gets the Boot*. (Tom is the cat, as in "tomcat," of course!) Tom and Jerry have been incredibly popular in movies, on television, and on video.

Created by William Hanna and Joseph Barbera, Tom and Jerry have been so well liked that they have had their own Saturday morning television series in each of the last four decades. Their first show ran from 1965 to 1972. There was another from 1975 to 1978. A third ran from 1980 to 1982, and then there was a *Tom and Jerry Kids Show* that aired from 1990 through 1993.

Tom and Jerry's longevity even resulted in their own feature film musical, made in 1993. *Tom and Jerry: The Movie* had songs created by top motion picture composer Henry Mancini. In this film, the cartoon cat and mouse actually talk and sing, which they had never done before, thanks to the voices of Charlotte Rae, Rip Taylor, Dana Hill, and others. However, most critics agreed that these audible additions were not improvements, preferring the original cartoons instead.

CATS IN ANIMATED FILMS AND TELEVISION, PART II: GARFIELD AND HEATHCLIFF

In more contemporary times, Garfield has been perhaps the most popular cat in comic-strip pages around the globe, as well as in his well-received television cartoon specials.

This fat and funny feline was created by Jim Davis in 1978, and starred in the first of his prime-time animated shows in 1982. Starting in 1988, Garfield became a staple of the Saturday morning cartoon lineup, where he remained as a regular in *Garfield and Friends* through 1995. On this show, Garfield's voice was supplied by Lorenzo Music, who had also found fame as the voice of Carlton the Doorman on the television series *Rhoda*.

In his specials and television series, Garfield has had many animated adventures, including "Garfield Goes Hollywood," where the wisecracking cat tries out for stardom on a show called

"Pet Search"; "Garfield in Paradise," in which he takes a vacation to a tropical island; and "Garfield: His 9 Lives," where he dreams about his past, present, and future lives.

Heathcliff is another popular comic-strip and cartoon cat. He has appeared on the big screen in *Heathcliff: The Movie*, which was a full-length, animated film actually pieced together from episodes of his cartoon television series, which appeared for many years on Saturday mornings. Heathcliff also appears on video, including various compilations put together from his television series. These videos include "Heathcliff & Cats & Co.," "Heathcliff's Double & Other Tails," and "Heathcliff and Marmaduke," in which the feisty feline teams up with the comic-strip Great Dane, Marmaduke.

CATS IN ANIMATED FILMS AND TELEVISION, PART III: TOP CAT, FELIX THE CAT, AND THE CAT IN THE HAT

Top Cat, the flinty feline who lived in a Manhattan garbage can, was first seen as the star of a prime-time television cartoon series, *Top*

Cat, during the 1961–1962 season. The show then moved to Saturday mornings.

Inspired by the creative antics of comedian Phil Silvers, Top Cat was surrounded by numerous henchcats, including Benny the Ball, Choo-Choo, the Brain, Spook, and Fancy-Fancy. Arnold Stang supplied the voice of Top Cat. There was a revival of *Top Cat* in the eighties, which took the savvy cat from his New York alley to Beverly Hills when he received an unexpected inheritance.

Felix the Cat is another animated feline on the silver screen who has been popular for many decades. Felix has gotten into an amazing number of adventures in hundreds of short subject films that first appeared in movie houses and now continue to pop up on television as well.

Dr. Seuss's famous *Cat in the Hat* has also had numerous cartoon incarnations, including an acclaimed television special in 1972. Numerous cartoon sequels have followed the show business debut of the freeloading feline, and this classic cat continues to be incredibly popular.

CATS IN ANIMATED FILMS AND TELEVISION, PART IV: WALDO KITTY, CATTANOOGA CATS, AND OTHERS

In the 1970s, there was an animated television series called *The Secret Lives of Waldo Kitty*, which was a Saturday morning takeoff on the famed James Thurber character of Walter Mitty. Waldo Kitty is a daydreaming cat who constantly gets into tussles with a pesky bulldog. In a creative twist, the animals are seen in live-action sequences, while Kitty's dream fantasies are cartoons. Some of these clever adventures have been repackaged under the title of *That's My Hero!* and can be found on video.

In addition to all of the animated felines who have filled the Saturday morning television line-up, there were also the *Cattanooga Cats*. These were actually live cats who, from 1969 through 1971, introduced animal-themed cartoon segments, including the popular Motormouse, who later got his own show.

On the big screen, cats were the villains in the 1986 animated musical film, *An American Tail*, which was produced by Steven

Spielberg. This popular feature tells the story of the cartoon mouse, Fievel, as a young Russian rodent who emigrates to America in the 1880s. He is exploited as cheap labor by his employer cats, but ultimately learns how to survive and triumph in the new land. Featuring voices of Dom DeLuise, Madeline Kahn, and Christopher Plummer, among others, the movie was also highlighted by the top-selling song, "Somewhere Out There."

In 1987 a creative, cat-themed cartoon titled *Cat City* was made in Hungary. In this James Bond spoof, the hero is a mouse who has to defuse a war-like weapon created by a group of evil cats. This animated motion picture has been dubbed into English and is available on videocassette.

MORRIS, THE CAT KING OF COMMERCIALS, PART I

Perhaps the most famous cat in the history of show business is Morris the Cat, the orange "spokesfeline" who sold millions of cans of 9-Lives cat food.

And Morris's rags-to-riches saga easily could have been a movie of its own!

Morris was a stray discovered in 1968 by noted animal trainer Bob Martwick at the Humane Society animal shelter in Hinsdale, Illinois. Morris was stuck in a tiny cage, scheduled to be put to death. Martwick had been on a talent search for an animal to make a commercial for a mattress manufacturer. He saw the giant, orange tabby, was smitten, and paid $5 for the cat's release.

Morris was actually called Lucky—an appropriate name considering his probable fate—until later that same year when he beat out many other cats to appear in an advertising campaign for 9-Lives. In fact, the producers of the commercial were so impressed with the poised and charismatic cat that they rewrote the ads so that Morris would be the star!

The results turned out to be phenomenal, and Morris became a cultural icon.

MORRIS, THE CAT KING OF COMMERCIALS, PART II

When commercials appeared starring Morris as the finicky cat who would eat nothing but 9-Lives cat food, the former stray became a sensational success!

This ad campaign continued for many years, and Morris won a special Patsy Award in 1973 for his "outstanding performance in a TV commercial." He also had roles in such movies as *Shamus* with Burt Reynolds and Dyan Cannon.

Morris became the toast of the town. He appeared on many television shows, was often seen with Hollywood stars, and even appeared at the White House, where he signed a bill by having his paw dipped in ink and making an impression on the paper.

Morris made an impression in

corporate boardrooms as well. He was named as an honorary director of Star-Kist Foods Inc., which owned 9-Lives, and was even able to give a "paws-down" on new cat food flavors developed by the company if he didn't like them!

Even with all of his success, Morris remained a friendly, cool—and very lucky—cat until he died in 1978.

LITTLE-KNOWN
FACTS ABOUT CATS

Cats may not have supernatural powers, as people once believed, but they do have abilities we don't completely understand—including the power to seemingly predict earthquakes. Some cat owners say that, shortly before quakes, their pets begin to run around in frantic agitation, bolting outside to hide at the first opportunity. In the hours just before a quake, mother cats have been known to move whole litters of kittens outdoors. Scientists think these cats are responding to subtle signs of rising tension around the geological faults where earthquakes occur. Cats may be able to sense early tremors while they're still too faint for humans to pick up. They may be responding to static electricity, which increases sharply just before a quake, or they may sense shifts in the earth's magnetic field. Cats also show some of the

same agitated behavior just before volcanic eruptions and severe storms. Researchers are
studying this phenomenon in
the hope that we may someday
be able to use our cats' pre-
science to protect ourselves
from natural disasters.

Can your cat
keep you healthy?
Don't laugh.
Science suggests
that if you own a
cat, you may live
longer. Research has found that
cat owners have lower rates of
minor health problems like in-

somnia, colds, flu, backaches, headaches, and fatigue. Cats have been used in psychiatric therapy, where they can help mentally ill people release tension and learn to form healthy relationships. Some progressive nursing homes allow their residents to own cats, finding that elders are healthier when cats give them the pleasure of physical contact and the comfort of affectionate relationships.

How do cats enhance our health? Partly, it's the simple pleasure of touch. Studies have shown that the act of stroking a cat relaxes a person's muscles and calms the whole body. And partly, it's the reassurance that comes from giving and receiving love.

Cats are some of the sleepiest members of the animal kingdom. They doze twice as much as humans do, averaging sixteen hours of catnapping in every twenty-four-hour period. Unlike people, who ordinarily stay awake through the daylight hours and do all their sleeping in one long session at night, cats sleep around the clock in relatively short bursts. This sleep pattern has evolved from the cat's efficiency as a hunter. Unlike other, less ferocious beasts, a cat can hunt for its food so quickly and effectively that it has ample time left over for snoozing. Cats experience three types of sleep. Brief catnaps last only a few minutes. In light sleep, a cat may doze for perhaps half an hour. During its deepest sleep, a cat will drowse for several hours, experiencing cyclical  shifts between light sleep and deeper sleep until it's ready to awaken. During the deeper phases of sleep, cats quiver, twitch, vocalize, and show rapid-eye movements that suggest they are dreaming.

Cats fall asleep more readily than almost any other mammal. But a cat whose diet is short in the amino acid L-tryptophan, found in milk, eggs, and poultry, may lose the ability to drop off naturally. Without this nutrient, a cat will become a jittery feline insomniac!

We've all heard stories about cats who find their way home across improbable distances, turning up at their own back doors weeks after disappearing miles away.

But are these tales true? Science has determined that cats do, indeed, have an innate ability to find their way home. One researcher borrowed pet cats from their owners, shut them in closed boxes, and drove them out of town on a winding, indirect route. He put the cats into an enclosed maze, with many exits located at the points of the compass. In significant numbers, the cats chose the exits that pointed in the compass direction of their homes. When researchers then repeated the tests, they drugged the cats first so that they couldn't possibly remember the twists and turns they'd taken on their journey. These cats, too, unerringly oriented themselves toward home. Scientists have attached powerful magnets to cats in the maze, and the cats lost the ability to find the right way out. Cats, therefore, use Earth's magnetic field as a giant compass, responding to signals from iron particles embedded in their living tissue.

Why do some cats love to play with catnip toys, while others can't be bothered? Some cats have a genetic sensitivity to *hepetalactone*, the active ingredient in catnip, but others don't. More than 50 percent of adult cats respond to the spicy-smelling herb with a ten-minute frenzy of pleasure. They lick, chew, and claw the catnip, rub their heads and bodies against it and roll in it, while purring, meowing, and even jumping with what looks like sheer delight. The rest of the cat population simply ignores the stuff. Catnip (*Nepata cataria*) apparently affects the brains of sensitive cats by "turning them on," just as some drugs affect people.

The response shows up in lions and other members of the cat family too. But kittens don't care about catnip until they reach the age of two or three months.

Catnip-sensitive cats may show a burst of uninhibited behavior in response to a few other plants, including valerian. But if your cat doesn't play with the catnip mouse you gave her for Christmas, toss it out, or give it to a friend with a more susceptible pet. Cats are either born with catnip sensitivity or they're not. It's in their genes!

The old saying "A cat always lands on its feet" isn't quite true. A cat can be injured or killed in a fall, just like any other living creature. But our feline friends have had to depend for centuries on tree-climbing to hunt for their food. In response, they've evolved a powerful righting reflex that dramatically increases their chances of landing safely in a fall. In a fraction of a second, a falling cat twists automatically through stages that researchers have identified through slow-motion photography. First, the cat's head rotates as the front legs move close below the fragile face to protect it from impact. Next, the spine twists, lining up the cat's front half with its upright head. Last, the hind legs bend up to match the forelegs while the rear half of the body finishes twisting. Just before touching down, all four legs stretch toward the ground, and the cat arches its spine to absorb the shock of impact. Throughout this twisting process, the cat's stiff tail rotates like a rudder, counterbalancing the weight of the body. This righting reflex happens so fast that in most

falls, cats do land safely on their soft, shock-absorbing paws, scampering off unhurt even from terrifying tumbles.

Are cats color-blind? Scientists once believed that cats saw the world in shades of gray. Now, they know that cats do see color—but not very well. Studies have shown that cats can distinguish among many colors, including red, green, gray, blue, and yellow. But felines are so sensitive to color value—that is, the relative darkness or lightness of a color—that they may not be able to tell two different col-

ors apart if both colors have the same level of grayness. That's how scientists were first misled into believing that cats couldn't see color at all.

Cats need sensitivity to relative brightness because their eyes are adapted to seeing in dim light. They're able to perceive movement and shape in much less light than people can. But cats don't need color to see in low-light conditions. That's probably why they don't seem to perceive colors with the intensity and sensitivity of their human companions.

Human eyes don't glow in the dark. So why do your cat's eyes shine like two green lanterns in your backyard at night? Cats' eyes don't glow with their own light, but they do have a special layer at the back of their eyes that is designed specifically to reflect light. It's called the *tapetum lucidum*, which means "bright carpet." This layer works just like a mirror at the back of the cat's eyeball, reflecting every trace of light that enters the cat's eye back toward the retina. With the help of this "bright carpet," cats are able to use all the light that's available to help them see movement and objects. Your cat can't see in absolute darkness any more than you can. To perform its light-enhancing magic trick, the *tapetum lucidum* has to have *some* available light.

Cats seem to be able to see in the dark because, in addition to their wonderfully light-adapted eyes, they use nonvisual signals from their ears, noses, and whiskers to navigate in darkness. Still, because of the structure of their eyes, cats can see shape and movement even in light so dim that their human owners are nearly helpless.

What's in a name? The word *cat* has a similar sound in languages all over the world, from the French *chat* to Italian *gatto* to *quttah* in Arabic. The Maltese say *qattus*, the Icelandic *kottur*. In Greek, a cat is *gata*, in Polish, *kot*, in Welsh, *cath*, and in Czech, *kocka*. Finns say *katti* or *kissa*. The *k* sound in all those words shows up even in countries where languages spring from different roots from the tongues spoken in Europe. In Africa,

Swahili speakers call cats *paka*. Speakers of Hindustani in India say *katas*. A Japanese cat is *neko*, and a Korean kitty is *koyangee*. Even our nicknames for our feline friends have international roots. Tabby cats probably get their name from *attabi*, a type of watered silk from Baghdad marked with wavering bars of color, like a cat's stripes. Our word *puss* may come from the name of an ancient Egyptian goddess, Pasht. Or it might derive from the old Irish-Gaelic *puus*, a word that probably began as an attempt to imitate the sound of a spitting cat.

A cat has about twenty-four movable whiskers, twelve on each side of its nose. Whiskers are more than twice as thick as ordinary hairs, and their roots are set three times deeper than hairs in a cat's tissue. Richly supplied with nerve endings, whiskers give cats extraordinarily detailed information about air movements, air pressure, and anything they touch. The scientific word for whiskers is *vibrissae*, a name that suggests their exquisite sensitivity to vibrations in air currents. As air swirls and eddies around objects, whiskers vibrate too. Cats use messages in these vibrations to sense the presence, size, and shape of obstacles without seeing or touching them. Whiskers are also good hunting tools. A cat whose whiskers have been damaged may bite the wrong part of a mouse it's attacking, indicating that signals from these delicate structures provide cats with vital information about the shape and activity of its prey.

Cats don't have facial expressions. Instead, their whole bodies show their feelings. A cat whose pupils are round may be frightened or excited, while an angry cat will narrow its pupils to threatening slits. A cat's whiskers swing forward when it is curious, threatening, or exploring. But if whiskers point backward, their feline owner is probably feeling defensive or trying to avoid touching something. Ears also signal feeling. The ears of a relaxed cat point slightly outward, but an alert cat's ears swing fully forward to point straight ahead. Upset cats may twitch their ears, and a cat under attack will flatten its ears fully against its head—a protective posture that helps to shield these fragile structures in fights.

Tails tell tales of feelings too. A bristly tail signals a furious or frightened cat. An upset cat may twitch its tail from side to side, indicating that the cat is feeling frustrated and torn between two choices—perhaps deciding whether to run for shelter or to fight back. Attackers will do well to avoid any cat whose ears are rotated backward but not fully flattened. This cat is signaling that it is furiously angry, but not yet scared enough to protect its ears by flattening them. In other words, this cat's ears are shouting a serious warning: "Watch out!"

Your cat will probably live longer than your grandmother's kitty did. A cat's life expectancy today is sixteen to eighteen years, more than twice as long as it was in the 1930s. The oldest cat on record, called Puss, died in 1939. As cat life expectancy grows, Puss may soon lose his spot in the record books. Already, at least one modern-day kitty is pressing hard on his tail. Granpa Rexs Allen, a show cat from Texas, reached the ripe old age of thirty-two in 1997. Granpa is almost bald, but his fur didn't fall out as a result of advanced age. Instead, he's been short on fur all his life because he's half-Sphynx, a breed of cat that's born hairless. His owner says that Granpa's advanced age may result from his unusual dietary preferences. This cat likes to eat broccoli! But don't start paring vegetables in the hope of extending your favorite kitty's life span. A vegetarian diet may be good for people, but it is hazardous to a cat's health. Anyway, most cats aren't nearly as fond of vegetables as long-lived Granpa. Their owners are likely to have trouble convincing them that a few extra years are worth the bother of broccoli.

Have you counted your cat's claws lately? Most cats have four toes on their hind feet and five on the front. But some cats have extra toes—as many as seven or eight on one foot! These cats are called *polydactyl*, from the Greek *polus* (many) and *daktulos* (finger). A polydactyl cat may have extra toes on just one of its feet, or on two, three, or all four of them. The extra toes result from a dominant gene that expresses itself differently in different cats. Most common on the forepaws, extra toes may not develop completely. Cats who have eight extra toes also sometimes have internal problems associated with high mortality. But most polydactyl cats are perfectly healthy. Polydactyl cats first appeared in Boston, spreading from there to Newfoundland,

Nova Scotia, and the rest of New England, where they're still common today. Sailors used to believe that cats with extra toes were good luck. By carrying them on board on their world-wide journeys, ship captains helped to disperse polydactyl cats across the seven seas.

A cat of a different color—green!—appeared in Denmark in 1996. Miss Greeny, a two-month-old kitten, was completely covered with grass-colored fur except for a gray spot on her back. Suspecting that the leafy tint wasn't natural, veterinarians tried to wash the green out of Miss Greeny's fur. But it wouldn't come out! On closer inspection, they discovered that the green color extended into the follicles below Miss Greeny's skin.

A cat's color is normally determined by its genes. The colors orange and black, for instance, are each carried on the X chromosome. Since male cats only have one X chromosome, they

can't ordinarily be calico (a mix of orange and black). A few male calico cats have turned up, though they're very rare. These cats are likely to have an extra X chromosome, and they're also probably sterile.

Miss Greeny's owner, Pia Bischoff, told Danish newspapers that vets thought her kitten's decidedly different shade could be caused by a metabolic disorder. But except for the unusual tint of her fur, Miss Greeny seems to be perfectly healthy and normal.

If you see a white cat with blue eyes, don't bother to call, "Kitty,

kitty, kitty." Chances are, the cat can't hear you. Most white cats with two blue eyes are deaf. If just one of a white cat's eyes are blue, the cat is likely to be deaf in the ear closest to the blue eye. And if the cat's eyes are orange, it probably has normal hearing. A white cat whose eyes have no color at all, causing a pink appearance when light reflects off the blood vessels in the eye, is an albino. In these cats, the pigment melanin, which gives color to skin and fur, is almost completely absent. No matter what color the rest of a cat's body is, if its ears are white, they'll be susceptible to sunburn. Just like fair-skinned people who've soaked in the sun too often, white cat ears are at risk of skin cancer. If you have a white-eared cat, use sunscreen to protect its vulnerable skin, or keep your cat inside, away from the damaging rays of the sun.

Counting cats is a tough job. Researchers estimate that between 57 and 67 million cats live in the United States. There are at least 3 million cats in Canada, 7 million in Great Britain, 35 million in western Europe, and 12 million in Australia. But nobody knows how many cats live in Africa, Asia, and South America. What's more, cat counters can't agree on *how* to count cats. Felines are often counted by keeping track of the amount of cat food purchased in a country over a period of time, rather than by counting the kitties themselves.

In the United States, for instance, cat owners spend $2.15 billion on cat food in an average year, dropping another $250 million to buy cat litter. This method is effective for counting pets, but it leaves out the millions of stray cats all over the

world who support themselves without help from humans. When researchers try to count these cats, they run into another disagreement: When is a stray a stray? Some cat counters include cats who live in cities, eating human garbage, but exclude feral cats who live with no human contact at all. Others count all unowned cats, stray or feral. The reality is that nobody knows for sure how many cats are alive on Earth today. But researchers do agree that cat numbers are increasing. That's why humane societies urge cat owners to neuter their pets, unless they're certain they can find a willing owner for every kitten in a litter.

Cats are popular pets in most countries. But in Australia, they've become Public Enemy Number One. There were no cats at all in Australia until European colonists imported them as they settled the isolated continent more than 200 years ago. With no cats preying on them, the continent's native species evolved without the natural ability to protect themselves from feline ferocity. Now, about 12 million cats call Australia home. These immigrant felines have been so successful at hunting lyrebirds, woylies, boodies, and other native animals that they've driven some species to near-extinction. To save Australia's unique species, many of whom exist nowhere else on Earth, one politician has called for the total eradication of all cats in the country by the year 2000. There's even a new slogan: "Do Australia a favor—kill a cat." Not all Australians agree that cats have to go. Instead, cat lovers are working for reasonable precautions, like neutering, that should allow responsible cat ownership while also protecting Australia's precious native animals. A 1991 law requiring household cats to be kept indoors has already helped the lyrebird population. But so many stray cats still hunt vulnerable Australian wildlife that it remains to be seen whether cats and kangaroos will ever coexist peacefully Down Under.

Scent defines a cat's world much

as vision defines ours. A cat's exquisite sensitivity to scent is one of the reasons you'll often see your cat wash herself thoroughly right after you've petted her. When you stroke your cat, sweat glands in your hands transfer your scent to your cat, covering up her own. Even though your cat may love to be handled, she does not like smelling "wrong." After a petting session, she won't feel fully comfortable until she has fixed matters by making sure she smells like herself again. She may also enjoy tasting you, as she licks your scent carefully off every square inch of her fur.

Cats are territorial creatures who know where they belong. The size of your cat's range depends on where you live, how much you feed your pet, and whether your cat is a male or a female. Male cats cover about ten times as much ground as females do. In the country, a male farm cat may hunt, explore, and lay claim to 150 acres of land, while females limit themselves to a range of fifteen acres on average. Wild cats range farthest of all, covering territories up to 175 acres. But ur-

ban cats limit themselves to much smaller territories than their rural counterparts. Cats in crowded cities may never leave an area of about one-fifth of an acre around their homes. An urban pet cat may define its territory by the size of its own

backyard. Re-
searchers have
established that
stray city cats
range farther
than their pam-
pered pet
cousins, showing that a cat's ter-
ritory shrinks in direct propor-
tion to how much food is
provided by its owner.

Female cats' territories may
overlap, with shared neutral areas where cats can meet without conflict. Male cats are less
likely to share portions of their
territories with other male cats.
But a male cat's territory *will* in-

clude the ranges of several females, allowing the male to
check on every member of his
harem as he pads through his
daily rounds.

FUNNY, AMAZING, AND TRUE CAT TALES

RESCUE ME!

Who says cats have no compassion toward dogs? The Los Angeles S. P. C. A. gave an award to Thug, a tomcat, for saving the life of a dog. Missy the Labrador was in danger of drowning under a pier when Thug saw her and began to howl. Her cries got the attention of nearby people, who pulled the dog from the water and saved her life.

NOT WHAT HE WANTED TO HEAR!

A friend of Dorothy Parker's was upset to find out that his cat was terminally ill and would need to be put down. He wondered aloud, "How could I possibly kill my cat?" Parker, a writer well known for her witty remarks, then replied: "Have you tried curiosity?"

HE CHANGED HIS TUNE

Harrison Weir attended and wrote about the world's first cat show, held at London's Crystal Palace in 1871. En route to the show, he met a friend who, hearing where Weir was off to, spent some time berating felines. Weir somehow convinced the man to accompany him to the cat show.

A few months later, Weir visited his friend, only to find him in the company of two happy, sleeping cats. Apparently, the cat show had impressed the former cat hater!

CATS 1, BIRDS 0

When Adlai Stevenson was governor of Illinois, he once vetoed a bill to keep cats from wandering out of their owners' yards and, thereby, killing birds. He didn't believe it was possible to legislate a change in cats' behavior, saying,: "[It is the] na-

ture of cats to do a certain amount of unescorted roaming. The problem of cat versus bird is as old as time."

BOMBS AWAY!

Cat ears can detect sounds with higher frequencies than human

ears can. In World War II England, cats would become agitated before bombs landed near
their owners' homes. Families
learned that once their cat became upset, it meant another
attack was on the way, so they
knew it was time to slip into the
bomb shelter.

CANARY-GATE?

Timmie the cat belonged to
a Washington newspaperman,
Bascom Timmons, in the 1920s.
Timmons used to take the kitty
to the White House for visits
with President Coolidge and his

canary, Caruso. Caruso and Timmie got along famously. Caruso would walk across Timmie's back, singing as he went, and he would even rest in the cat's paws. Eventually, the president gave Caruso to Timmons.

BREAKING THE CODE

A Los Angeles Siamese, Missy, liked to run across her owner's computer keyboard, perhaps to chase the mouse. One day, she pawed a combination of letters that turned out to be a code that deleted $50,000 worth of files from a local business's com-

puter. The company had to repair its entire computer system.

NEWTON'S FIRST LAW . . .
OF CATS

Sir Isaac Newton, English physi-
cist and mathematician, cut an
opening in the bottom of a door
in his house so his cat could pass
in and out at will. When the cat
had kittens, Newton made a
smaller hole next to the original
one.

THAT ENGINE PURRS LIKE A KITTEN

Imagine Jerry Ditzig's surprise when he pulled two mewing kittens out of the engine of his boat. Before the Bud Lite International Outboard Grand Prix in Missouri, he was doing practice laps when he discovered the wet stowaways, who were later named, appropriately, Speed and Racer.

DO YOU TAKE CREAM IN YOUR CAT?

A White House guest who was

breakfasting with President Calvin Coolidge was surprised to see his host pour some coffee into a saucer, then add milk and sugar. Thinking he ought to follow etiquette, the guest began to pour his own coffee into a saucer. When he looked up, the president had placed the warm drink on the floor for the White House cat.

TASTES LIKE CHICKEN

Imprisoned by Henry VIII in the tower of London, Sir Henry Wyatt was close to starvation until his cat showed up at his cell with a pigeon for him to dine on.

A SWEET TRIBUTE

British prime minister Winston Churchill adored his cat Jock, whom he received for his eighty-eighth birthday. Jock lived at Chartwell, Churchill's famous home, for years after his master died. There was a clause in Churchill's will that stipulated that a marmalade cat shall always be kept at Chartwell; he also left a nice sum of money to cover room and board for all the "Jocks" that would live after the original. The house is open to the public, where visitors can see the present Jock look-alike.

MIGHTY MOUSER

Mickie, a cat employed as a mouser for Shepherd and Son Ltd. in Lancashire, England, is reported to have caught more than 22,000 mice while on patrol for the business from 1945 to 1968.

THAT'S THE WAY THE COOKIE . . . WANDERS

Dogs usually get all the credit for being able to find their way home after getting lost, or finding their owner's new house during a move. However, in December

1949, Cookie the cat proved that felines have quite good navigational instincts too. Cookie got shipped (accidentally, we hope) from her home in Chicago to Wilber, Nebraska, 550 miles away. Then six months later, she was back on the doorstep in Chicago.

KITTY IN THE CORNER POCKET

Mark Twain, self-proclaimed cat lover, had a kitten that liked to snuggle itself into a corner pocket of Twain's billiard table. From there, it would watch— and disrupt—the game by batting at the billiard balls.

THE GREATEST SHOW IN FUR

Englishman Leoni Clarke had a troupe of fifty performing cats. These acrobatic felines walked on tightropes, stepping over arrangements of mice, rats, and canaries. They also jumped through flaming hoops.

THAT'LL BUY A LOT OF CAT FOOD!

It's not totally unheard-of for cats to inherit estates and large bank accounts when a wealthy owner dies. Take Hellcat and Brownie, for instance. In the 1960s, these two lucky pusses received almost half a million dollars from their owner's estate.

BELIEVE IT OR NOT

Cats are the most popular pets in America! They surpassed their canine contenders in popularity during the mid-1980s. According to the latest estimates, there are more than 66 million pet cats in the United States as opposed to approximately 58 million dogs. This means that nearly one in three American households has a pampered puss in it.

Americans don't have a term for a mixed-breed cat (in other words, the feline equivalent of a mutt)! But in England they call their nonpedigreed cats "moggies." Perhaps this name will catch on in America?

A whopping 95 percent of cat owners talk to their cats!

Many of the worst dictators in history were also cat haters. Hitler, Mussolini, Napoleon, and

Genghis Khan are all said to have been enemies of felines—and they didn't seem to fare any better with people. Perhaps cat-hating should be considered a sign . . .

A one-year-old cat is considered to be the age equivalent of a sixteen-year-old human. However, this ratio does not stay the same through their life spans. A twelve-year-old cat is approximately the same age as a sixty-four-year-old person, while a twenty-two-year-old cat would be 104 in people years!

Owning a cat can lower your blood pressure, cut your cholesterol level, and possibly even save you from a heart attack. According to a University of Pennsylvania study, doctors found that petting a cat can reduce both a human's heart rate and blood pressure. Researchers have also shown that the survival rate for heart patients with pets is considerably higher than for those who have no animal companionship.

The most popular names for cats today are said to be Tiger and Samantha.

In China, there actually are seismologists with cats who use their furry friends to save thousands of lives. For instance, in 1975 in Haicheng, China, these scientists saw their cats acting in a strange manner and then alerted city officials to evacuate the area. Twenty-four hours later, a devastating earthquake hit and caused tremendous damage—which would have been a lot worse had it not been for the warning.

Nobody knows for certain what makes a cat purr! Some scientists believe that the sound comes from false vocal cords, which are a bundle of membranes that are located near the cat's actual vocal cords.

Other researchers think purring originates from the vibrations of the hyoid apparatus, a series of small bones that connects the cat's skull to its larynx, and that also helps to support its tongue.

Still others believe that purring

is created by the pressure of a cat's blood as it passes through its chest. There is another group that insists the sound comes from the puss's voice box when its mouth is closed.

Even though the reason is still unknown, a cat's purring is one of the most pleasing sounds a pet lover can hear. However, owners should know that cats don't just purr when they're happy. In fact, cats will purr for many reasons—even when they are hurt or frightened. For instance, by purring, a cat may try to pacify an enemy animal.

Cats that live indoors tend to live twice as long as cats that are allowed to go outside. With all the dangers from traffic, diseases, and other animals, being out and about can end up curtailing a kitty's life.

Chocolate can be fatal to your feline. It may be mouthwatering to you, but your dandy dessert contains oxalic acid and alkaloid theobromine, both of which can be very harmful to your kitty.

The average mass-produced cat meal is equivalent in quantity to five mice! (Yum.)

Most felines dislike orange and lemon rinds. This can be a boon to you if your curious cat likes to dig its paws into your furniture. Rubbing an orange rind on your furniture will often dissuade your puss from using it as a scratching post.

Some male cats will rub up to certain shampoos and hand creams in your medicine chest! This is because they contain an ingredient called methylparaben—which has a scent resembling a female feline in heat.

Cat hairs *do* stick to your clothes more than the hair of almost any other animal! There are a number of reasons for this. One is that a cat's hair is considered to be the most electrostatic. Another is that a cat has three types of hairs. They have primary hairs with microscopic barbs on them that make them more susceptible to sticking to clothes. They also have "awn" hairs that tend to be rough and clingy. Finally, they have secondary hairs that, because they are so thin, easily get caught in the rougher fibers of most human clothing.

The result? Hairy clothes!

It's possible that, unlike humans, most cats are left-pawed! There has not been much research on this subject, but in tests, a majority of cats seem to have a noticeable preference for using one paw more than the other. And of that majority, two-thirds prefer to use their left paw instead of their right to reach for food.

Cats *do* have belly buttons! Even though felines are born from amniotic sacs, they have belly buttons that are, in essence, a scar located next to the rib cage. However, because most cats have so much fur, these are often very hard to see.

All kittens are born deaf, blind— and with blue eyes! Their sense of hearing comes quickly as they grow, while their sight will usually develop completely in about a month and a half. Their eye color will change over the course of their first four months of life. Cats have three eyelids! This third lid is called a nictitating membrane, which helps to keep your kitty's eyes moist.

Cats have such great hearing that they can tell your footsteps are approaching—from hundreds of feet away! Your puss also seems to have perfect pitch and will often leave the room when a singer or musician is performing off-key. (Everybody's a critic!)

You should *never* trim a cat's whiskers. Intrepid felines need them to find their way in the dark or to figure out how they can get into—or out of—tight spots.

You shouldn't give most cats a bath. Some soaps can remove a feline's important natural oils. Water can also chill the cat, leaving it vulnerable to sickness.

Many cats will try to get your attention when you are talking on the telephone because they do not see anyone else in the room and think you are talking to them!

There once was a talking cat! Peter Alupka was known as "The Wonder Cat" when he performed in the 1920s with the Circus Busch in Berlin, Germany. This cat had been taught to cry out names such as "Helen" and "Anna," to sing along with songs, and to cry out "Hurrah!" at the end of his act.

In fact, this conversational cat was so famous that his performance was recorded.

There *have* been flying cats—in a manner of speaking. According to *The Cat Name Companion*, by Mark Bryant, a California cat in the 1920s is said to have jumped on a duck's back and flown in the air until the scared duck landed again. And supposedly in 1939, a cat in Turkey was picked up by an eagle who soared away and then dropped the poor puss from a great height. However, except for a broken leg and a clipped tail, the cat survived and soon recovered from its unexpected flight.

Some cats are said to have wings. Over the course of the century, photographs have been taken of winged cats on both sides of the Atlantic Ocean. One such cat is

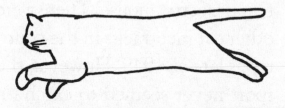

said to have been killed after swooping down on a child in Sweden in 1949. The documentation of such cats, however, is about as reliable as the "proof" of the Loch Ness Monster.

There were once cat-racing tracks in England! In fact, the first official cat racetrack opened in Dorset, in 1936. This track was a 220-yard circuit, and more than fifty felines would chase after an electric mouse. There were other cat racetracks in the country as late as 1949. However, the sport never seemed to catch on like horse or dog racing.

A cat was once elected to the student senate of Southern Illi-

nois University in September 1971. The cat, D. E. Gordon Oltman, won the election on a platform concerning the problem of stray dogs roaming the campus. This political puss was actually entered in the campaign by its owner, Diane Oltman, to prove that students paid little attention to the way they cast their votes.

The expression that someone "let the cat out of the bag" actually has a lot to do with pigs. In medieval times, pigs were often stuffed into burlap bags when they were sold at fairs. Because customers could not see what they were buying, they might—and often did—end up with a cat instead of a pig!

The only way they would know for certain is when they "let it out of the bag."

The expression that it is "raining cats and dogs" comes from a country where there seems to be as much snow as rain!

In Norse legends, animals were supposed to have magic powers. For instance, cats were rumored to be able to create storms. Dogs were symbols of wind. Hence, in Scandinavia, when it was "raining cats and dogs," it meant there was a violent storm full of wind and rain.

The legend that a cat has nine lives is said to have come from the ancient Egyptians, who were amazed at how cats could survive falls from great heights unscathed.

There is a breed of cat that looks like a dog. The Peke-faced Persian has very canine-like characteristics. Many cats through the ages have had doggy propensities: It is said that the ancient Egyptians would use cats when they went hunting, much as dogs are used today. Images of felines retrieving prey have been found on several relics and tombs in Egypt.

The hairless cat is not really hairless! The Sphynx cat seems to have no hair, but actually is covered in a very fine layer of fur.

There is a word in the English language if you suffer from the delusion that you are a cat. It is *galeanthropy*.

According to *The Whole Kitty Catalog* by John Avalon Reed, our feline friends are subject to some pretty strange laws in the United States.

For instance, cats in Idaho are legally prohibited from joining in a fight between two dogs.

In Dallas, any cat running in the street after sundown must wear a headlight.

In Lemonine, Montana, cats must wear three bells to warn birds of their approach.

In Morrisburg, Louisiana, cats may not chase ducks down city streets.

In Natchez, Mississippi, cats are forbidden to drink beer.

WELL-BRED CATS

THE SPOTTED EGYPTIAN MAU

In Egyptian, "mau" means "cat." Some trace the Mau's ancestry back to the ancient cats pictured in Egyptian temples and revered as gods. Others claim that the Mau's resemblance is only a result of selective breeding. In either case, the Mau is the only naturally spotted domestic breed.

This medium-size, shorthaired cat has soft, silky fur. Its banded legs and tail, the barred M on its forehead, and gooseberry-green eyes give it a distinctive appearance. But years of inbreeding have created health problems:

heart disease, knee problems, and missing limbs.

Although the Mau is gentle and affectionate with its own family, it may be shy or aloof with strangers. Alert and observant, these cats will often chirp to warn their owners of a stranger's approach.

THE ACTIVE, AGILE ABYSSINIAN (AB-AH-SIN-EE-AN)

The Abyssinian probably originated near the Indian Ocean or in Southeast Asia, not in Abyssinia (now Ethiopia). When

British soldiers left Abyssinia in 1868, they brought some of these cats home. Soon, the British were importing them from Abyssinia.

The first of this breed arrived in the United States in the early 1900s. Americans fell in love with this graceful-looking cat with long, slender legs and neck. Its soft, silky fur lies close to its body. Each hair has alternating dark and light bands, tipped with the darker color, giving the coat a ticked effect.

This intelligent cat can be trained to do stunts. Abyssinians appear in television commercials and movies. They love company and will follow their owners around the house. Although they make great companions, Abyssinians aren't lap cats—they're explorers. These fearless cats love high places, such as banisters and refrigerators. There's never a dull moment with an Abyssinian in the house.

SAVED FROM EXTINCTION: THE TURKISH ANGORA

For centuries, Turkish Angoras roamed the region of Angora, now Ankara, the Turkish capital. They first arrived in Europe in the 1600s. Early in the twentieth century, indiscriminate breeding virtually eliminated them as a breed. But in 1962, American servicemen discovered Turkish Angoras in the Ankara Zoo. Back in the forties, zoo officials had started their own breeding program to prevent the extinction of one of their national treasures.

This small- to medium-size longhaired cat has a long, lithe body. Unlike any other breed, the Angora carries its plumelike tail horizontally over its body, with the tail's tip brushing its neck. The very fine hairs of the Angora's single coat shimmer as it walks.

These affectionate, gentle cats often choose one or two special family members to whom they devote much of their attention. They prefer a calm household where someone makes sure the cat's eating area and litter box are spotless.

TURKISH VAN:
THE SWIMMING CAT

This ancient breed probably originated in central and southwest Asia. It's thought that the breed took its name from Lake Van (pronounced "Von") located in southeastern Turkey. In

1955, two British women vacationing in Turkey returned home with two Turkish Van kittens, starting this breed's development in Great Britain. Nearly thirty years later, Vans arrived in the United States.

Turkish Vans are white, semi-longhaired cats with distinctive markings on their head, ears, and bushy tail. This piebald pattern in other breeds is called the Van pattern. Their soft, silky coat is waterproof. These big, broad cats often grow to be three feet long.

Unlike other domestic breeds, Vans love to swim. If a lake or stream isn't available, they'll settle for a sink or tub. At home, they're affectionate and enjoy amusing themselves with toys, playing hide-and-seek, and retrieving.

THE PLACID PERSIAN

These longhaired cats may have originated in Persia (now called Iran), but hieroglyphic references to similar cats, dating from 1684 B.C., cast some doubt on that assumption. But, whatever their origin, there's no doubt that the Persian is the most popular longhaired breed.

Long-term breeding has changed its original look. Today's modern Persian has a massive head with a round, flat face that looks as if someone pushed in on its short snub nose. The traditional "doll-faced" Persian has a more moderate-looking head with a normal nose. Both have short, squat, stout bodies with thick, woolly coats. Their dense undercoat causes the outer coat—which can grow up to six inches long—to fluff out from the body.

This luxurious coat needs daily maintenance, but these placid cats won't mind sitting still for their grooming. Although some Persians remain playful into adulthood, most prefer to lounge and sleep. Their quiet, gentle manner makes them perfect indoor cats.

THE GOOD LUCK KORAT

In Thailand, the Korat symbolizes wealth and good luck. This silvery blue cat's Thai name is Si-Sawat (see-sah-what). *Si* means "color" and *sawat* is a wild fruit with a silvery blue seed. When presented with a Si-Sawat, King Rama V of Siam (now Thailand) named it the

Korat after the province from which it came.

The Korat's short, blue fur lies close to its body. Silver tipping on each hair makes the coat shine. This sweet, gentle cat has a heart-shaped face with huge round eyes that change from blue to amber to luminous green as it ages.

When first placed in a home, the Korat forms strong bonds with one or two family members. From them, this cat demands attention. The lap-loving Korat enjoys petting. Strangers, sudden noises, and boisterous pets and children scare them, so the Korat does best in a quiet, orderly home.

THE ROYAL CATS OF SIAM: THE SIAMESE

The world first learned about this cat when the royal family of

Siam (now Thailand) gave pairs as gifts to visiting dignitaries. Although these cats had roamed the royal rooms of Siam for centuries, they may have originated elsewhere. The Siamese people called them "Chinese cats." When these handsome cats arrived in Europe in the late 1800s and in the United States in the early 1900s, people clamored for more.

Heavily built, with round heads and small ears, these early Siamese were called "apple-heads" and are now referred to as "traditional" Siamese. Early breeders bred for length. The resulting "classic" Siamese had a longer head, body, and legs. Breeders didn't stop there. Modern Siamese have extremely slender bodies with long, narrow heads and huge flared ears. These "extreme" Siamese are mainly show cats because their personalities are as extreme as their appearance.

All Siamese are "pointed cats." Their pale-colored bodies have darker colors on their points: face, ears, legs, and tail. The original point colors were seal (dark brown), chocolate (milk chocolate), blue (bluish gray), and lilac (pinkish gray).

Their short, silky coat enhances their long, graceful look. The crowning touch on these beautiful cats is their slanted, almond-shaped eyes that shine a deep, sapphire blue.

Siamese are loudmouths. Experiments reveal that they use eleven consonants and all the vowels in their vocalizations. They're fastidious, fussy cats with strong opinions and an independent will that drives some people crazy and endears them to others. The latter appreciate their affectionate, intelligent personality. Their nimble paws can empty drawers and flush toilets. For people who crave a talkative, cuddly companion, the Siamese is the perfect cat.

BIRMAN: THE SACRED CAT OF BURMA

In Burma, many believe that the souls of departed priests return to their temples in the form of Birman cats. Natural breeding between shorthaired Siamese and long-haired, free-running cats may explain the origin of these long-haired, pointed cats. In 1919, a pair of Birmans were shipped to France. The male died en route, but the pregnant female survived to start this breed in the Western world.

This large, blue-eyed cat has a light-colored, longhaired coat with a darker color marking its face, legs, and tail—its "points." A silky ruff surrounds its neck. Unlike other pointed cats, the Birman has four distinctively white paws.

Birmans are quiet, dignified cats that don't demand attention. They'll happily play by themselves while their owner is busy. They're active, but not athletic, so they don't tend to get into trouble. These easygoing cats do well in multiple-pet households.

THE BECKONING BOBTAILS OF JAPAN

Stylized, ceramic statues of Japanese Bobtails with one paw raised in welcome sit in the doorways and windows of many Japanese homes and stores. These "good luck" Japanese cats first arrived from China or Korea more than a thousand years ago.

This small- to medium-size

cat's three-inch tail is as unique
to it as a set of fin-
gerprints. Each tail
is distinctly kinked,
curved, notched,
and/or angled. The tail hairs grow
out in all directions, resembling a
pom-pom. The Japanese favor
Bobtails with brilliant red and
black patches on white. This col-
or combination is called *mi-ke*
(MEE-kay), Japanese for "three-
furred."

These talkative cats respond
to human conversation with
chirps, hums, clicks, and chants.
Their fearless adaptability and
sweet tempers make them excel-

lent travelers and children's pets. However, this active, strong-willed cat requires companionship and activity or it may behave destructively.

SKOGKATT: THE NORWEGIAN FOREST CAT

For centuries, this hardy, long-haired cat stalked the vermin of Scandinavian farms. It's thought that *Skogatt*, as they are known in their native land, might have resulted from interbreeding between shorthaired cats left by the Vikings and longhaired cats brought by the returning Crusaders. On their own in the forests, they developed the characteristics necessary for survival in the harsh northern environment.

The Skogkatt's thick, water-repellent outercoat shields against rain and snow. Its woolly undercoat insulates from the cold. A thick ruff and full bib protect its neck and chest. While waiting for prey, this hunter covers its feet with its thick, bushy tail. Long tufts of hair on its wide paws create miniature snowshoes. Three- to four-inch hairs in the ears protect against frostbite.

Although these large cats love the outdoors, they do well as indoor cats if given adequate room and a climbing tree. They're gentle, friendly, intelligent, and soft-spoken.

THE ARCHANGEL CAT: RUSSIAN BLUE

Legend holds that Russian czars kept these cats. When the czar exiled former friends, their Russian Blues traveled with them to such faraway places as Arkhangelsk, located on the White Sea, roughly 150 miles south of the Arctic Circle. Six

hundred years ago, ships visiting this far northern seaport picked up these regal cats and brought them to distant shores. That's how they received their name: the Archangel Cat.

How did this shorthaired cat survive the Arctic cold? The Blue's fur stands out from his body in a plush, double coat and has been compared to the coat of the seal and beaver. Tips of silver on each gray-blue hair give the coat a lustrous sheen. This coat plus vivid green eyes make the Russian Blue a handsome cat.

In the days of the czars, Russian Blues were trained to jump through hoops and somersault. Today, these intelligent cats open doors and enjoy playing fetch. And when attention isn't available, the undemanding Blue will entertain itself.

THE CALM, CONTENTED BRITISH SHORTHAIR

Nearly 2,000 years ago, Roman soldiers brought domestic cats to Britain. Natural breeding among these cats produced several varieties, one of them being the British Shorthair. Through the ages, the British have valued them as rodent exterminators.

Round describes this large, stocky cat. The Brit's chubby, round cheeks and curved-up lips inspired the Cheshire cat's smile in *Alice in Wonderland*. Of all cats, the British Shorthair probably has the densest coat. Blue-gray is the most popular color, but Brits come in many colors and patterns.

Although young Brits like to play, adults prefer to lie around and sleep. Nothing bothers the placid British Shorthair, not even large dogs. These peaceful, quiet cats are easy to live with. Because they're a favorite with animal trainers, they've appeared in numerous films and television commercials. This is the perfect cat for the busy family with little time to fuss over the cat.

THE BLUE CATS OF FRANCE: CHARTREUX (SHAR-TROO)

Roman crusaders returning from Turkey and Iran may have brought the Chartreux's ancestors to France. Whatever their origin, these blue-gray cats have wandered the French countryside for centuries. Commoners prized them for their hunting abilities and pelts.

Their soft, dense, blue-gray coat is woolly and water repellent. Slightly longer than most shorthair coats, it stands out from their body. Silver tipping gives it a sheen. The strong, sturdy Chartreux are large cats, with males weighing up to sixteen pounds. Because of their curved lips, these gentle giants always appear to be smiling.

The Chartreux's tiny voice is seldom heard. One breeder describes this feline as "slightly more talkative than a stuffed cat." That's indicative of their unassuming ways. They enjoy being with people, but not underfoot. These tolerant, gentle cats make good travelers, and they don't mind being left alone for long periods of time.

THE TAILLESS MANX

Spontaneous mutations resulting in tailless cats have occurred throughout the centuries and around the world. However, when this mutated gene occurred or arrived hundreds of years ago on the small, isolated Isle of Man off the coast of England, it perpetuated itself, creating the famous Manx breed.

Not all of these round-looking, shorthaired cats are tailless. "Rumpies" are the truly tailless cats. "Risers" have a small knob, while "Stumpies" have a movable stump. Fully tailed Manx are essential for healthy breeding since the gene responsible for the taillessness is lethal when doubled. "Rumpies" shouldn't be bred together. Tailed Manx are rarely seen since breeders dock the kittens' tails to avoid a painful arthritic condition in adult cats that often requires the tail's amputation.

Like dogs, Manx retrieve objects, follow their owner, bury their toys, and growl at suspicious noises. If let outdoors, they're dedicated hunters, but these even-tempered cats make perfectly contented indoor pets as well.

AMERICAN SHORTHAIR: THE "ALL-AMERICAN" WORKING CAT

The ships carrying the first settlers to the New World had cats on board to kill the shipboard rats. When the passengers disembarked, so did the cats. On land, they worked as farm cats. In the late 1800s, Siamese and Persians mated with these cats, producing a mixed breed. Alarmed that this would be the end of the American

Shorthair, some breeders began selective breeding to preserve this uniquely American cat.

Although "mixed-breed" cats often resemble the American Shorthair, differences exist. A litter of mixed-breed cats may contain short- and longhaired kittens having different temperaments. A litter of American Shorthairs contains only shorthaired kittens with quiet, sweet dispositions.

Easygoing American Shorthairs adapt to any living situation from the barn to the apartment. Their hard, protective coats come in more than eighty different colors and patterns. Although most don't enjoy cuddling, they'll purr contentedly, curled up beside their owner's feet.

MAINE'S STATE CAT: THE MAINE COON

America's only naturally occurring longhaired breed probably evolved from the first settlers' domestic shorthaired cats and free-running longhaired cats. The longhairs may have been seafaring cats that jumped ship or cats the Vikings introduced to the New World. Natural selection and Maine's harsh climate created this large, rugged breed.

The Coon's long, shaggy coat

resists water and provides warmth. The large paws act as snowshoes. Thick tufts of hair protect the cat's ears from frostbite. Its resemblance to a raccoon earned this breed its name: Black stripes ring the Maine Coon's tail, and the cat's most common color, brown tabby, resembles the raccoon's coloring.

Like raccoons, Maine Coons are intelligent and agile. They like to jump and climb, and are superior hunters and playful clowns. Even older Coons act like kittens, willingly playing fetch or chasing marbles. These even-tempered cats make great pets for active families with children.

THE DRAIN CATS OF SINGAPORE: THE SINGAPURA (SIN-GA-POO-RA)

The Singapura roamed Singapore's streets, fending for themselves and taking refuge in the gutters, earning them the name "drain cats." An American working in Singapore brought some back to the United States in the seventies, and breeding efforts began shortly thereafter.

This smallest of the cats weighs six pounds or less. It has

a ticked coat of dark brown against an ivory background. Very large ears and eyes give it an expressive, alert look. Singapuras have an unusual gait; like lions, they move with a sinuous, rolling amble.

The Singapura's compact size and silky coat make it irresistible for hugging. Although this feline is affectionate with its own family and follows them

around the house, it's shy with strangers. The Singapura loves curling up in warm places: on laps, near heating ducts, in spots of sunshine, and under blankets. When it's not cuddling, this inquisitive cat can be found exploring all the home's high places.

BURMESE: THE SMILING CLOWNS

Wong Mau, a sable-brown cat, arrived in the United States in the 1930s from Burma. Her owner mated her with a Seal Point Siamese. Over time, selective breeding of Wong Mau and her kittens resulted in a new breed, the Burmese.

These medium-size cats carry a lot of weight for their size and have been called "bricks wrapped in silk." *Round* describes their heads, feet, chests, eyes, and even their ear tips. Their thick whisker pads and tipped-up mouth corners make them appear as if they're always smiling.

These clowns entertain with their acrobatics and mischievous tricks. They drape themselves around necks and perch atop shoulders. These attention-loving cats curl up in laps or snuggle next to their owner in bed. Since the Burmese have few survival instincts, they need to be kept inside. That can be difficult, however, as these escape artists rival Houdini.

HAVANA BROWNS: THE CONSTANT COMPANIONS

In the 1950s, English breeders set out to develop a brown, Siamese-built cat. They crossed a Siamese with mixed-ancestry, black shorthairs to produce Havana Browns. Some insist this breed was named after a brown rabbit by that name. Others claim that the color they share with the Havana cigar inspired the name.

Their glassy-smooth, short-haired coat looks like polished mahogany and feels like mink. Each hair is brown from its root to its tip. Even this cat's whiskers are brown. Its green eyes, protruding corncob-shaped muzzle, and forward-tilting, large ears give the medium-size Havanas a distinct appearance.

These gentle cats enjoy constant physical contact and will ride around on people's shoulders or worm their way onto laps. When they feel ignored, they'll tap their owner gently with their paw to gain attention. Their quiet friendliness, as well as their front paw, is almost always offered to all.

THE BOMBAY: A PETITE PANTHER

In 1953, a Kentucky breeder set out to create a pantherlike cat. She crossed a grand champion Burmese with a black American Shorthair. After years of selective breeding, she succeeded in creating the Bombay, so named because of its resemblance to the black leopard of Bombay, India.

The Bombay's black-to-the-roots coat lies close to the body, shimmers like patent leather, and feels like satin. Its large, wide-set, gold to deep copper eyes shine like lights in the night. This muscular, small to medium-size cat is heavier than it looks.

These agile cats have no fear of heights. They enjoy playing with people and purr when held. Like dogs, Bombays fetch objects and

can be taught to walk on a leash.
These petite panthers will even
guard your house!

EXOTIC SHORTHAIR: THE BUSY PERSON'S PERSIAN

The breeding of Persians with
shorthaired cats such as the
Burmese, American, and British
Shorthairs, and even the
Russian Blue resulted in the cre-
ation of the Exotic Shorthair.
Today, only outcrossings with
Persians are allowed to maintain
this breed's standards.

Exotic Shorthairs look like
shorthaired Persians. They have

the same pushed-in face and short, chunky body. Their dense, plush, double coat stands out from their body and doesn't mat or tangle.

They're the perfect cat for the person who wants a Persian, but doesn't have the time to groom it. Like the Persian, Exotic Short-hairs are quiet, undemanding cats that enjoy sleeping. They're slightly more responsive and playful than Persians and, even as adults, enjoy jumping for a toy on a stick or batting a piece of paper across the floor.

ORIENTAL SHORTHAIRS: COLORFUL SIAMESE

Old books from Siam describe Siamese cats of other colors than the pointed, but since the Siamese Cat Club of Britain only allowed pointed Siamese in their competitions, breeders stopped breeding anything other than pointed Siamese. The other colors disappeared from the Siamese gene pool. In the 1950s, several breeders crossed Siamese with domestic shorthairs to see if they could bring back some of these other colors and patterns. These colorful Siamese were eventually named Oriental Shorthairs. Today, this breed boasts more than 300 different colors and patterns. All have the familiar Siamese build and personality.

THE CURLY CAT OF CORNWALL: THE CORNISH REX

In 1950, a spontaneous mutation created a long-limbed,
curly-coated male in a litter of
straight, shorthaired kittens. By
selectively breeding this male,
his owner produced more curly-
coated kittens. She named this
new breed "Cornish Rex" because of the similarity of its coat
to that of the "Rex" rabbit,
whose fur trimmed the royal

robes of King Henry VIII.

Large, flared ears sit atop the Rex's small, narrow head, giving this cat a "space alien" look. His curly coat feels silky soft, but doesn't hold in body heat. In order to stay warm, this cat's metabolism works harder and requires more food.

Muscular legs enable this athletic cat to jump high, start quickly, reverse directions in a flash, and chase at high speeds. This gymnast loves to wriggle into nooks and crannies. One breeder described these active, friendly cats as "slightly less lively than a hurricane."

THE DELIGHTFUL, DEVOTED DEVON REX

Ten years after the Cornish Rex mutation, a similar mutation occurred in Devonshire, England. A male kitten named Kirlee had a curly, black coat. When he was bred to Cornish Rex females, only straight-haired kittens resulted. Obviously, a different gene mutation had caused Kirlee's curly coat. From then on, each breed developed separately. Kirlee's descendants were named Devon Rex.

The Devon's batlike ears, prominent cheekbones, and

enormous wide-set eyes give it a pixielike appearance. Compared to the Cornish Rex, Devon Rex have a smaller build, and shorter, less wavy coats. Their rippling fur feels velvety soft.

Like the Cornish Rex, this breed requires additional food to stay warm. Not only are Devons enthusiastic eaters, but they adore unusual foods like asparagus and cantaloupe. These lively, intelligent cats want to be included in the family's activities. They enjoy cuddling in laps, snuggling in bed, and riding atop their owners' shoulders.

THE RAGDOLL: THE HEAVYWEIGHT OF PEDIGREED CATS

The crossing of Persian, Birman, and Burmese cats in the early 1960s resulted in the development of a longhaired, pointed hybrid, the Ragdoll. These cats earned their name because of their tendency to go as limp as ragdolls when held.

Ragdolls are large. Four-year-old males can weigh twenty pounds or more, and females weigh up to fifteen pounds. Their nonmatting, silky coat feels as soft as rabbit's fur.

Ragdoll kittens are all-white at birth. It takes two to three years for their coat markings to develop fully.

Because of the Ragdoll's docile personality, it doesn't require a huge space in which to live. This gentle cat tolerates almost anything. It loves to be stroked and cuddled. Like a puppy, it greets people at the door and follows them around the house. This nonaggressive cat lacks the instincts to defend itself, so it must be kept indoors.

OCICAT: THE HOMEMADE OCELOT

In the 1960s, a breeder crossed an Abyssinian with a Siamese. When she crossed one of those kittens with another Siamese, she obtained the cats she'd been hoping for, Abyssinian-pointed Siamese, and one surprise—a spotted kitten. Since it resembled an ocelot, her daughter called it an "ocicat." Other breeders liked this cat and simultaneously began breeding ocicats. Later, they were crossbred with American Shorthairs to increase their size and variety of colors.

Like the Abyssinian, contrasting colors band each hair. The hairs in the spots are tipped with the darker color. Its short, satiny coat is usually cinnamon, silver, tawny, or chocolate.

The gentle Ocicat loves to follow its owner around, but is not demanding. These intelligent cats are easily trained to respond to commands and walk on leashes, making them good travelers.

SOMALI: THE LONGHAIRED ABYSSINIAN

Now and then, a longhaired kitten would be born into a litter of shorthaired Abyssinians. Most breeders would quietly give away these "mistakes." In the 1960s, some breeders campaigned for acceptance of these longhaired siblings as a separate breed. Since "Longhaired Abyssinian" was dull, breeders suggested "Somali," for Somalia, the country bordering Ethiopia, formerly Abyssinia.

Sometimes called the "fox cat," the Somali has medium-length, ticked fur and a full, brush tail.

Like the fox, it moves swiftly and gracefully. They're slightly larger than the Abyssinian, but otherwise have the same lithe body, long legs, and alert look.

Somalis share the Abyssinian's intelligence, liveliness, and curiosity. Unlike the Abyssinian, they enjoy being on people, riding their shoulders or cuddling in their laps. They have no fear of strangers and see them as people to befriend.

BANNED IN BRITAIN: THE SCOTTISH FOLD

A Scottish farm cat gave birth in 1961. When the kittens were a few weeks old, a spontaneous mutation caused one of the kitten's ears to fold forward and down. She was the first Scottish Fold. Unfortunately, it was soon discovered that folded-ear cats had a high incidence of ear mites and deafness, among some other health problems, and the registries of Great Britain and Europe refused to register them. Although ethical breeders can avoid these problems, Scottish

Folds are still banned by England's official cat registry. United States registries recognized this new breed in the 1970s.

These medium-size cats have round bodies with round heads and large, round eyes. With folded ears, their wide-eyed expression reminds one of an owl. They can be either long- or shorthaired and have folded or straight ears.

Scottish Folds have many unusual behaviors, such as sleeping on their backs, sitting up on their haunches like prairie dogs, or sitting on their rumps with their back legs pointing forward.

These sweet-natured cats adore companionship and will supervise their owner's household activities.

THE ENERGETICALLY FRIENDLY TONKINESE

A Canadian breeder developed the Tonkinese in the 1960s and 1970s, by crossing a seal point Siamese with a sable Burmese.

This breed may have been around earlier, but wasn't recognized as a separate breed. It is thought that Wong Mau, the mother of all Burmese, was a Tonkinese.

This pointed cat has an intermediate build, not as stocky as the Burmese nor as slim as the Siamese. It reminds many of the traditional "apple-head" Siamese. Their fur lies close to their body and feels like mink. No other pedigreed breed has the aqua-colored eyes of the Tonkinese.

The gregarious Tonks demand attention from friends and strangers. Its sociability, plus adaptability, make it a great traveler. Famous for their acrobatics, they fearlessly leap from high spot to high spot in the house and tightrope-walk on the curtain rods. Some owners describe their Tonkinese as part puppy and part monkey.

SPHYNX: THE FURLESS PURR

Although reports of hairless cats go back at least a century, today's Sphynx breed traces its founding to hairless kittens born in Minnesota and Ontario in the mid-1970s. In both cases, a spontaneous mutation caused hairless kittens to be born to domestic shorthaired cats.

Sphynx appear hairless, but most have fine down over much of their body. Their skin feels like warm chamois. Two huge ears sit atop their small head. The Sphynx's muscular body has a pear-shaped appearance and ends with a whiplike tail.

This ultimate lap cat is famous for its neck hugs and face licks. Sphynx get along well with both pets and people. When not cuddling, they investigate cupboards or play fetch. No fur means they need to eat more food to maintain their body temperature. Since they have no coat to absorb their body oils, they require regular baths, or they'll leave oily spots on the furniture.

SUPERLATIVE KITTIES: THE BEST, BIGGEST, MOST POPULAR, AND MORE

BIG, FAT KITTY CATS

The heaviest domestic cat on record seems to be a porky puss named Himmy. Owned by Thomas Vyse of Cairns, Australia, Himmy tipped the scales at forty-six pounds, fifteen and a quarter ounces. With a fifteen-inch neck and thirty-three-inch waist, Himmy would have made a trim human, but he was one big cat!

Another feline fatty was a Welsh-born puss named Poppa who weighed in at forty-four and a half pounds. In the United States, the heavyweight champ is thought to be a forty-three-pound ginger-and-white tabby who lived in Connecticut.

On average, most domestic cats weigh somewhere between five

and seven pounds, although some breeds can weigh as much as twenty pounds. Of 330 breeds, the ragdoll is the heaviest, with males weighing in at an average of fifteen to twenty pounds.

ITSY, BITSY KITTIES

Talk about teeny kitties: a male named Ebony-Eb-Honey Cat weighed in at a mere one pound and twelve ounces in February 1984, when the small Siamese was already nearly two years old. He was owned by Angelina Johnston and lived in Boise, Idaho.

Tinker Toy, a male blue point Himalayan-Persian, was merely two and three quarter inches tall and only seven and a half inches long.

The smallest breed of domestic cats is the Singapura or "Drain Cat" of Singapore. The average adult male weighs a mere six pounds and adult females weigh in at a waifish four pounds.

WRINKLED PUSSES

Cats may have nine lives but we usually only measure one. The oldest cat on record is Puss. Said to have celebrated his thirty-sixth birthday on November 28, 1939, he then passed away peacefully the next day.

Another feline senior citizen was Ma, who was probably a great-great-great-grandma when she was put to sleep in 1957 at the ripe old age of thirty-four.

In the United States, a Los Angeles feline lived to be thirty-three years and four months before taking his final catnap. And Bobby, an Irish cat, was thirty-two years and three weeks old before he went up to kittycat heaven.

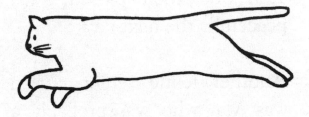

SPEED DEMONS

Over the distance of sixty yards, a cat was once recorded doing twenty-seven miles per hour. (Perhaps it needed to use the litter box?)

The speediest member of the entire cat family is the cheetah, which has been recorded at speeds of up to seventy miles per hour over a distance of 100 yards.

TELL ME A TAIL . . .

The cat with the longest tail is Pinky, who hailed from London. In 1978, his tremendous tail measured a whopping fourteen inches—and probably caused quite a breeze every time he flicked it!

ONE COOL KITTY

While most pusses want to

warm up to the fireplace, one breed actually *likes* the cold. The Norwegian Forest Cat has adapted to the frigid temperatures of Scandinavia. And even though this brawny breed has lived for thousands of years in the wild, it can also be perfectly content indoors.

ONE BUSY MAMA

Talk about a lot of litters—a cat named Dusty gave birth to her 420th kitten on June 12, 1952, at the age of seventeen!

Most female felines are able to have kittens until about the age of eleven (the equivalent of the human age of sixty). However, cats usually give birth to fewer kittens as they get older. Male cats as old as sixteen have been known to father litters, which is more than the human age of seventy!

A LOTTA MOUTHS TO FEED

The largest litter on record

(ouch!) consisted of nineteen kittens, which were delivered on August 7, 1970, to a very fertile feline named Tarawood Antigone, a Burmese cat who was four years old at the time. Unfortunately, four of the kittens were stillborn. Of the surviving fifteen, only one was a female.

HIGH-ALTITUDE TABBIES

A four-month-old kitten followed a group of climbers to the top of the 14,691-foot Matterhorn Mountain in the Alps on September 6, 1950.

Some other astounding instances of high-altitude tabbies:

In 1928, the members of a mountaineering club in the Swiss Alps were surprised when a cat showed up at the club's hut—which was a whopping 9,000 feet above sea level! The hutkeeper immediately adopted the cat, which made itself at home at the mountain retreat and often followed climbers up the craggy, frozen slopes to a peak that was more than 12,000 feet high.

In 1962, a kitten named Zizou moved in with a mountaineering club at the Albert Premier shelter at Mont Blanc in France, which is almost 9,000 feet high. Zizou liked to zigzag up the slopes with mountaineers to the peak—which is more than 15,000 feet into the clouds.

And in Yorkshire, England, a female cat was driven up the wall by a dog—literally—in 1980. Scared by the pooch, the kitty zoomed up some seventy feet to the roof of a five-story apartment building.

TABBY TAKES A TUMBLE

Patricia, a one-year-old pregnant puss, truly knows what a comedown is. This kitty seems to hold the world record for surviving a fall from the greatest height.

On March 8, 1981, she was thrown off St. John's Bridge in Portland, Oregon, and fell 205 feet into the whirling Willamette River. Two fishermen rescued injured Patricia and brought her to a vet. She was operated on, and although she lost her kittens, not only did she survive, she was adopted by a loving family that later displayed her proudly in cat shows.

Perhaps Patricia was able to survive her incredible tumble because, by spreading their legs and arching their backs as they fall, cats seem to make a natural parachute of themselves.

WELL-TRAVELED FELINES

According to *The Cat Name Companion* by Mark Bryant, during the course of sixteen years, a kitty named Princess Truman Tai-Tai logged in more than 1.5 million miles as a crew member of the British ship *Sagamire*.

Doodles, a regular aboard the ocean liner *Cedric*, also traveled more than a million miles in his seafaring career.

Up in the skies, a remarkable kitten took some tremendous flights during World War II. Members of the U.S. Fifth Air Force Division found him climbing aboard a cargo plane in Australia. With a face that looked a little like the German dictator, the kitty was christened Adolf. Adolf logged in almost 100,000 miles during many perilous combat flights. Once the engines started, the cat would appear just minutes before the plane took off—and would spend most flights sleeping peacefully near the plane's radio equipment.

CURIOSITY ALMOST KILLED THE CAT!

In 1983, an eight-year-old cat named Buttons got stuck under the hood of a car. Unfortunately, she was stuck there for six hours before being rescued at a gas station.

The cat was taken to a vet; when an airline found out about her misadventure, the frazzled feline flew home free of charge to be reunited with her owner—the neighbor of the driver.

FREQUENT FLYER

A black-and-white cat named Tom got lost in the hold of a British Airways jet and flew more than a half-million miles in two months. Before being rescued at Heathrow Airport by his owner, Tom visited such far-flung places as Australia, Canada, Jamaica, and Kuwait.

TREMENDOUS TREKS

The record for a feline finding the way to its owner's home is said to be held by Tom, who traveled an amazing 2,500 miles from St. Petersburg, Florida, to San Gabriel, California! This journey took Tom two years and six weeks—and, by the time he arrived in California, he was much the worse for wear. But the courageous cat was happy to be back with his owners again.

There have been other stories of felines finding their families after becoming separated during a move or a vacation.

In Australia, a Persian cat named Howie is said to have traveled 1,000 miles across the continent to find his teenage owner, after she and her family moved. It took the cat a year to traverse the rivers, deserts, and wilderness of the Australian Outback, but somehow he made it back to his owner.

MORE REUNIONS OF CAT AND OWNER

Other persistent pusses who have made tremendous treks to find their owners include a cat named Clementine who, in 1949, made her way from New York state to Denver, Colorado—a place she had never been—to find the family that had left her behind!

In 1953, a soldier from Indiana had taken his cat with him to his new base in Georgia. Shortly after, the cat disappeared. The disappointed military man searched for her to no avail. He later found out that in three weeks, the cat had made its way back to Indiana and was hanging around its former home.

And in 1955, a woman was

shocked to find that her persistent puss named Ling-Ling, whom she had left behind in the care of her sister, had somehow managed to travel from Sandusky, Ohio, to Orlando, Florida—an area that was completely foreign to him—to join her.

MARVELOUS MOUSERS

Rodents should have run from a female tortoiseshell cat named Towser, who was owned and employed by the Glenturret Distillery Ltd. of Scotland. By the age of twenty-two, she is credited with killing 28,899 mice, averaging three ravaged rodents per day.

WET BEHIND THE PAWS

A black-and-white Persian would regularly paddle between the ships in the harbor of St. Mary's in the Scilly Isles. He was also known to go swimming in the sea every evening to catch his dinner with his bare paws!

In fact, there are some breeds of cats that like water. These include the auburn-and-white Turkish Van cat as well as the Fishing Cat of Malaysia, India, and Sri Lanka. The latter actu-

ally has slightly webbed feet that
help it fish for its supper!

THEY'RE IN THE MONEY

Mark Bryant, in *The Cat Name
Companion*, tells of a number of
lucky cats who are in the money
because of generous owners
who predeceased them and left

a bounty of booty in their wills.

In 1992, a seven-year-old feline named Cyrus inherited an $850,000 mansion in Bridgeport, Connecticut, and the litter boxes (one in each of the fifty rooms) that went along with it.

An alley cat named Charlie

Chan was the sole recipient of a $250,000 estate. The will stipulated that the entire estate—which included a three-bedroom house, seven-acre pet cemetery, and collection of valuable antiques—should be auctioned off when Charlie Chan passed on, and the proceeds donated to a number of humane societies.

In 1991, a pair of Burmese named Damon and Pythias were the recipients of a $750,000 Manhattan co-op on Fifth Avenue—with a view, of course. The will required the cats' caretakers to give the friendly felines toys to play with and make sure that they got their hairball medicine.

Cat charities have also benefited from some wonderful wills. Three charities that support stray cats received an astounding $14 million from Ben Rea, an eccentric millionaire and miser. Britain's Royal Society for the Prevention of Cruelty to Animals will receive $5 million in exchange for taking care of a cat named Blackie. And in France, a couple of rich cat lovers donated a spectacular $60 million to charities that look after the country's abandoned felines.

PRICEY PUSS!

A California Spangled cat was purchased for $24,000 in January 1987 from the Neiman Marcus Christmas catalog. Quite a number of people feel that paying such a price for a cat is the ultimate in conspicuous consumption and is not in the animal's best interest.

In 1967 an English woman was offered $5,880 for her cat by an American breeder. Coylum Marcus, her copper-eyed white Persian, was an international champion. The woman refused to sell her cat, who kept her company for eleven more years.

PARTY ANIMAL

Certainly one of the most popular

cats of contemporary times was Tommy Clark, a yellow tomcat who lived in Seneca Falls, New York, during the 1930s.

On Tommy's twenty-third birthday, more than 700 cats attended his birthday party. The next year, more than 1,500 guests (felines and people) were invited—including President Franklin D. Roosevelt, who, alas, had to send his regrets.

FAN CLUBS

With more than 600 cat clubs throughout the United States, the largest cat organization in

the country is the Cat Fanciers'
Association, Inc.

SHOWY CATS

The largest cat show
ever held in the United
States attracted a record
1,200 feline participants.
Held on November
17 and 18, 1995, at
McCormick Place in
Chicago, the International Cat
Show was the place to be for cat
lovers!

The first cat show in America
took place on March 6, 1881, at
a museum on Broadway in New

York City. According to published reports of the time, the cats in question were not happy about being exhibited—there was much hissing, scratching, and clawing!

BELOVED PERSIANS

The most popular breed of cat in the United States is the Persian. According to the Cat Fanciers' Association, there are approximately 45,000 registered Persians in the country.

Rounding out the top ten most popular cat breeds in the United States are: Maine Coon, Siamese,

Abyssinian, Exotic, Oriental, Scottish Fold, American Shorthair, Birman, and Ocicat.

However, only a small percentage of house cats in America are pedigreed. Unlike dogs, who are often bred for their performance as working animals, cats are bred only for their good looks and temperaments.

CARE TIPS AND HELPFUL HINTS

Dry, crunchy food helps keep a cat's teeth healthy, but soft, moist food has the benefit of supplying water, which cats need. (Mice and birds, a staple of cats in the wild, are about 80 percent liquid—like humans.) A shortage of water in the diet is suspected of contributing to feline bladder problems. There-fore, whenever dry food is served, an ample supply of clean water should also be made avail-able.

For cats that have grown up eating dry food, drinking enough water is seldom a problem. They learned as kittens to drink water (or milk) in adequate quantities, and they maintain that pattern throughout their lives. A mature cat that is switched to dry food may not do so well, however. Cats are creatures of habit, and their habits may not include drinking water as a part of their daily rou-tine. A cat that fails to increase its water intake upon being switched to dry food may develop concentrated crystals in its urine, which can cause painful bladder inflammation and infection. Regular monitoring of fluid intake is important under these circumstances.

Although your cat is friendly and cuddly with you and your family, do not assume it will act cordially to the neighbor's cat or to another cat you introduce into its environment. Cats are essentially solitary creatures. They come together in nature for only one reason: sex. Otherwise, they view each other as competitors—for food, sex, or territory. Domesticated cats view humans, on the other hand, not as competitors but as providers of life's necessities. Humans don't mark turf the way cats do, nor do they (normally!) feed on local rodents and birds.

True, some cats—though by no means all—who live in the same human household will become fast friends and cuddle together adorably. This is because the abundance of food provided by their humans (along with neutering and spaying) blunts the normal competitive urge.

Even in these circumstances, however, another cat, especially an unfamiliar one, may well receive an extremely unfriendly reception.

More than a few people are allergic to cats, far more than are allergic to dogs. The problem is not necessarily cat hair itself. The more likely culprit is dead skin, which is sloughed off in the natural course of things, and cat saliva on the hair. One helpful step an allergic person can take is to brush the cat and cut its nails outside, so the skin and nails don't end up covering the floor and furniture. Another is to have a nonallergic person rub the cat frequently— several times daily, if possible— with a damp sponge, the goal

being to remove the saliva with which a cat coats itself in the course of its numerous daily baths.

Although they may eat vegetables and fruits from time to time, cats are true carnivores. In this respect, they differ from humans (and dogs), omnivores whose bodies are capable of converting plant life as well as animals into the nutrients essential to survival. It's fine if you and your family want to be vegetarians, but cats can acquire certain vital fats and amino acids only by consuming the bodies of other animals that have already manu-factured them.

Cats have little need for food other than meat. Note that when they eat their prey, they typically eat the entire thing—skin, bones, and internal organs, as well as muscle. The lesson for humans attempting to duplicate the cat's natural diet is that food served should contain 25 to 30 percent protein and 15 to 40 percent fat.

Cats want and need variety in their diet. Not only will they get bored with the same food day after day, but they can develop disease as a result of prolonged

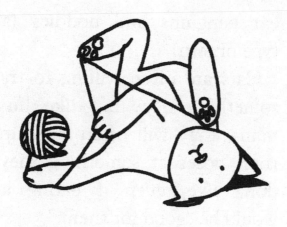

feeding on a single type of meat.

Note that cats throughout the world have widely varying diets. Cats in America consume lots of chipmunks. European cats thrive on mice and rabbits. Australian cats enjoy ring-tailed possum. Cats on certain islands eat penguins and noddies (a type of tern).

Cats are often willing to try something new, but like humans, they will often turn up their noses at something they don't like, even if eating it would be "good for them."

There is no point in trying to discourage your cat from raising its tail and sticking its rear end in your face—or in the face of your boss, who is visiting for the first time and whom you are desperate to impress! In the presence of those they trust, human or animal, cats carry their tails high and present their posteriors for inspection and sniffing as a means of acknowledging the other's superiority (or at least equality). Odor is very important in the cat world, and when a cat allows you to "capture" its odor, which is produced by two glands in the anal area, you are receiving a compliment not to be sneezed at.

Even the most finicky cat is likely to drink out of the toilet bowl, the sink, or a dripping tap. This is not inherently worrisome. Drinking from a dripping tap or even a running hose is simply more fun than drinking from the same old bowl every day. Tap water may also taste better than water that has been sitting out in a bowl for any length of time. Also, some believe that cats evolved with a preference for moving water because in the wild they found that stagnant ponds and the like were unsafe.

If your cat drinks from alternative sources, the challenge for you is to make sure those sources are safe. Toilet bowls may contain toxic cleaning chemicals, and plant vases may contain poisonous residue of plants.

Note that if you deliberately leave the tap dripping to ensure that your cat has an adequate water supply (some people do this when they go out of town for a day or two), behavior that began out of curiosity may become a habit that is difficult to break.

The normal cat has thirty teeth, the nature of which clearly reflects their development as carnivores. The knifelike canine teeth, in particular, are ideally suited to clasping prey and tearing flesh.

Because of how their teeth are constructed, cats cannot chew food. They are able, however, to perform cutting or slicing. Therefore, any food served to a cat should be chopped up or at least served in lumps small enough that a cat can get its mouth around it for purposes of tearing it into digestible pieces.

While some veterinarians advise against ever serving a cat food with bones, others believe that the only bones to watch out for are fish bones, which have a tendency to get caught in a cat's throat. Vets of the latter opinion point out that cats in the wild are hardly known to leave tidy piles of mouse or bird bones after each meal. (One thing cats do typically avoid, however, is feathers.)

Do not worry if your cat eats grass (unless you have a really big cat and a really small lawn!). This is natural. Cats eat grass mainly to facilitate throwing up furballs and other ingested but indigestible items, but also be-

cause they occasionally enjoy a "salad."

Outdoor cats often prefer one type of grass over another, just as humans prefer one type of veg-etable over another. Typically, the preference is for young, succulent grasses, over older, drier forms.

If your cat is eating grass, the most important thing for you to do is make sure that any fertilizer or pesticides you use on your lawn are nontoxic.

Vomiting furballs is a perfectly natural function for cats. It is less than pleasing from an aesthetic viewpoint, however, and the output can stain rugs and furniture. There are a couple of things you can do to reduce the frequency of such incidents.

First, note that a cat's fur lengthens in the winter and

shortens in the summer—which means that the longer winter hair will begin coming out as spring arrives, typically aided by the cat's grooming process. This tendency is much more pronounced in the outdoor cat; the indoor cat engages in hair removal throughout the year. It is also more pronounced in the longhaired cat, which is more likely to develop furballs in its stomach rather than pass the hair through its intestines.

It is good to brush your cat regularly to rid it of excess hair, and this is especially true during the molting season. Also, there are products you can feed your cat that will assist its intestines in passing the hair along with other waste, rather than vomiting it onto your favorite sofa. Consult your veterinarian about the latest options. Finally, if you are really concerned about this, make your next cat a short-haired one.

If you are disappointed in your cat's performance as a mouser, the problem may rest with you. The better you feed your cat, the less likely it is to be a good hunter.

Some level of stalking urge is innate in cats, but generally a kitten must be taught to hunt. Thus, if its mother was not a hunter, or if it was removed from its mother very soon after birth, the kitten will probably never learn to hunt and may be incapable of surviving in the wild.

Interestingly, some cats occupy an intermediate ground. They know how to hunt and seem to enjoy it, but the local humans feed them so well that they don't really need to hunt for food. Hence the notorious

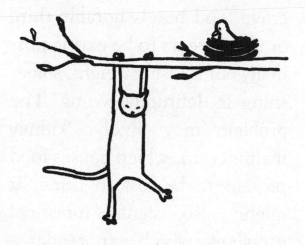

tendency of some cats to vanquish local prey and then do nothing with it (other than leave it conspicuously on the doorstep, apparently as a present for humans).

If your cat constantly seems to

crave food but is notably thin, or if it appears to be eating normally but is losing weight, something is definitely wrong. The problem may involve kidney malfunction, which causes food protein to be lost in urine. It might also signal intestinal problems, which can render a cat unable to digest the nutrients in its food. In this situation, the cat is literally starving, although its food intake appears optimal.

Increased appetite and/or weight loss might even indicate an overactive thyroid gland, which causes the body's metabolic rate to increase, raising the cat's daily energy requirements and also causing it to become jumpy and high-strung.

All of these problems are amenable to treatment, but because the treatments will vary depending on the core problem, immediate consultation with a capable veterinarian is in order.

If your cat ever exhibits a marked increase in thirst, and there is no obvious explanation, such as a change from moist food to dry, you should assume that something is seriously wrong.

Kidney malfunction is the most likely culprit. Kidney problems are often treatable by a measure as simple as putting the cat on a low-protein diet, either through one of the commercially available low-protein foods designed specifically for cats with kidney problems or through dilution of the cat's normal protein source with something like rice.

Diabetes can also manifest itself through heavy water intake. In this situation, insulin injections may be necessary.

Other possible explanations include: fever, anemia, bladder

infection, and the side effects of some medication the cat may be taking. In any event, immediate consultation with a veterinarian is mandatory.

There are various good reasons for your cat to turn up its nose at food, most having nothing to do with the oft-cited feline tendency to be fickle. For one thing, a cat's acute sense of smell en-ables it to detect chemicals, food deterioration, and other repugnant odors that humans are incapable of discerning. Toxic products used to "clean" the cat's food bowl, for example, may escape your notice but be obvious to your cat. Any impairment of a cat's sense of smell, such as an upper-respiratory infection, may induce it to stop eating altogether, because it cannot smell the food.

A cat's appetite may also be reduced by sores on its mouth or tongue, or by environmental disturbances, such as unfamiliar noises or unusual levels of light.

A cat may also refuse food that is too cold, preferring its  victuals at room temperature.

A number of foods that are acceptable or even highly beneficial for a cat are not acceptable on an exclusive basis. If you feed a cat nothing but liver, its bowels may become upset. If you feed it nothing but lean meat, it may experience calcium and other deficiencies. A diet consisting heavily of raw fish may lead to a vitamin B_1 deficiency, due to an enzyme in fish that destroys that vitamin and could also transmit tapeworms. A solution to both fish problems is simply to cook it (and make sure to remove any bones).

Eggs are a bit more complex. Uncooked egg whites destroy certain types of vitamins. Egg whites that are cooked, while safe enough, have no nutritional value. The best approach with eggs is to feed the cat only the yolks, raw or cooked.

Do not feed your cat dog food. There is a difference—beyond the fact that one type of food is labeled "Cat" and the other "Dog." Perhaps most important, cat food has more meat. This is because cats *need* more meat. Also, dog food has ingredients that cats cannot digest. In this respect, among others, dogs more closely resemble pigs than cats do.

When buying cat food, look for compliance with guidelines set by the Association of American Feed Control Officials (A. A. F. C. O.), a nonprofit group made up of federal and state officials. The February 1998 issue of *Consumer Reports* discusses cat (and dog) food at length and analyzes a number of specific, commercially available brands. Some highlights of that issue: (a) Dry food is typically cheaper (per day) than canned food; (b) if your cat has been thriving on a given food for, say, the last six years, there's no need to change to a "senior" food; (c) any food that meets the A. A. F. C. O. nutrition requirements, whether labeled "lite," "low calorie," or something else along those lines, must be capable of maintaining the animal's current weight. Thus, you'll have to feed it smaller quantities.

Under standards set by the Association of American Feed Control Officials, cat food that is labeled, for example, "beef cat food," must contain at least 95 percent beef (minus the water

used in processing), whereas a food that is labeled "*with* beef" need not contain more than 3 percent beef. An in-between label—"beef *dinner*" (or "platter" or "meal") must have at least 25 percent of the indicated food product.

When buying a cat, you're probably going to pay top dollar at a pet shop, and the animal you get may well come from one of the large, commercial breeders who sometimes separate kittens and their mothers too early and pay inadequate attention to socialization. Also, young cats are especially vulnerable to infection and illness, which are more likely to spread in the comparatively crowded conditions at some pet stores.

Your best bet is to go to a reputable breeder who raises the cats at home. You can find breeders at cat shows, or you could check *Cat Fancy* magazine. A purebred cat may cost from $250 to $1,000, depending on factors such as the rarity of the breed.

Alternatively, you could adopt a cat from the local humane society or the Society for Prevention of Cruelty to Animals, where you might pay anything from zero up to $50, which often includes the first round of shots, an initial health checkup, and spaying or neutering.

Feeding a stray kitten milk is a classic gesture of compassion. The problem is that cat's milk is different from cow milk. The former has more protein and fat. Also, some cats can't tolerate cow milk and will develop diarrhea.

When feeding kittens whose mother is for some reason unable to provide milk (the mom may have died, or she may be neglectful or physically impaired), there are several options. One is evaporated milk, prepared at up to twice the normal concentration (one-half the water) as that used for humans. Another is baby-milk formula, also prepared at up to twice the normal strength used for human babies. Also, there are commercially available cat milk substitutes (usually in powder form, requiring the addition of water).

Finally, for cats of any age that are sensitive to milk (or, to be precise, the lactose in milk), one remedy may be simply to dilute the milk with water, carefully monitoring the cat's waste output for negative reactions. And cats that will eat yogurt and similar products should be permitted to do so, because the lactose in these has already been chemically broken down.

There are several good reasons for spaying or neutering a cat not intended for breeding. As for males, the unneutered cat may wander, get into fights (which can lead to disease, not to mention bloody wounds and hostile neighbors), and mark its territory by spraying strong-smelling urine on rugs and furniture. As for females, the unspayed cat is likely not only to turn up with unwanted pregnancies but also to generate strong interest in unwanted visitors.

When obtaining a cat, check it yourself, looking for various things. First, go for one that appears friendly and amenable to human handling. If you're looking at kittens, go for the bolder one, the first one to venture toward your outstretched hand. Whatever the age, its coat should be smooth, unmatted, and free of ticks, fleas, and other creatures. Its ears should be dry and wax-free. Its nose should be damp, its mouth pink, its teeth white, and its anal area clean (and otherwise free of signs of diarrhea). Watch it walk around a bit, checking the cat for signs of lameness.

Any new cat, especially one you're planning to allow outside on a regular basis, should be kept inside for at least a few days—better yet, a full week. The goal is to give the cat a sense of your place as its home, the place it should return to from its explorations. You can promote this goal by fussing over it as much as possible in the first week, spoiling it with special tidbits, minimizing environmental irritations (e.g., don't begin home renovations the very next day), and so on.

When you finally let your cat out, be sure it is wearing a tag with your name and phone number. Escort it on its first outings, and make sure to get it back inside before nightfall.

All the guidelines regarding the introduction of a new cat to your home are equally applicable when you and your old cat are moving to a new home. First, keep it inside for at least several days. You don't want it to go out and immediately begin searching for its old home.

Also, retain as many elements of the old and familiar as possible. Keep all its toys, its favorite blanket, its usual brand of food. Don't change its brand of litter or the litter box itself. You would even do well to keep at least a portion of semiused litter in the box. Cats are highly sensitive to smell, and nothing will give it a sense of being "home" more than the aroma of its own urine.

When lifting a grown cat, be sure to support its weight at both ends. Do not utilize the classic approach of small children, which is to grab it under its front legs and leave the rest of it dangling.

As tempting as it is to cradle a cat like a baby, with its tummy facing up, note that some cats do not enjoy this position and will struggle and even bite to get away.

When lifting a kitten, don't pick it up by the scruff of its neck, the way you might have seen its mother doing. A mother cat has the benefit of thousands of years of evolution to make sure she does this correctly. When handling kittens, note that their rib cages are highly delicate and bruise easily.

If you're planning to separate a kitten from its mother, do not—except under special circumstances—do so until the kitten is at least six weeks old. Better yet, wait eight weeks, when it is fully weaned from mother's milk.

It is good to begin picking up kittens, however, around three weeks after birth (some veterinarians say six weeks), to accustom them to handling. Have visitors pick them up, too, to accustom them to a variety of human hands and scents. The latter point is especially important if you are planning either to show your cat or to place it with a new family (rather than keep it). In either case, your cat will benefit from becoming used to handling by unfamiliar people.

Cats are notorious for choosing their own places to sleep. You could set up a custom-made, color-coordinated kitty house with a four-poster bed, complete with mattress, box springs, and heating pad, and your cat might end up spending the night in a cardboard box.

It might also end up spending the night with you. If you like this, or at least don't mind it, there is no problem. If you find that it cramps your style, however, you should establish an alternate routine as soon as possible, ideally from the moment the cat first enters your house.

Begin the routine by putting the cat in its own "room," fully equipped with litter box and food and water (or at least water), just before you go to bed. Make sure the room is warm enough, by using either a radiator (or the like) or an electric blanket or heating pad. Ideally, the room will have space both close to the heat source and further away, so the cat can choose a warmer or a cooler location, depending on its own needs and preferences.

Finally, close the door and brace yourself for some heartrending protests. If you're lucky, the room will be far enough from your bedroom that the crying won't keep you up all night. In any event, it should end in a week or two.

Cats need exercise. The typical outdoor cat gets plenty from its normal routine of hunting, climbing, exploring, and so on. The indoor cat can get enough from climbing on furniture and playing with toys, but you should help it out in this regard as much as possible. You can do this, first, by introducing it to toys (and play) early on, thereby accustoming it to running, jumping, and rolling around inside. You can also help by providing it with climbing and scratching posts, as well as an ample supply of toys, perhaps rotating the toys that you leave out from week to week so as to prevent the cat from getting bored by seeing the same things lying around all day. Any personal time you can put in throwing a cloth ball or wiggling a feather-on-a-wire toy of course helps.

If you live in a high-rise apartment or for some other reason are planning to keep your cat indoors, you're better off starting with a kitten (or, next best, a cat that has always lived indoors). Cats that are used to hunting, wandering widely, and enjoying the other stimulations of an outdoor life do not adapt as well to indoor life as those that grew up in it.

Similarly, if you're going to get two cats, you're better off getting two kittens, because cats that have not yet reached puberty are more likely to get along than two with all the sexual and territorial drives that puberty triggers.

You don't often see a cat on a leash. There is a reason for this: It is hard, if not impossible, to get a cat to walk on a leash like a dog. If you're to have any chance of success with this method, you are well advised to start early, with a weaned kitten. The sooner you familiarize the kitten with both the collar and the leash, the better your chances. Start off with short walks, preferably around familiar areas, and depending on the results, branch out from there.

Certain breeds, such as the Siamese, appear more amenable to leashes than others, but you may find that your particular cat will never go for it. In no event should you drag your cat on a leash against its will. This won't achieve compliance and only risks hurting him.

A cat that literally never goes outside can get by without a collar, but a cat that goes outside even just occasionally should definitely have a collar and a tag with your address and phone number. This is also a good idea for a cat that lives in a house where people, especially children, go in and out often. Lots of cats lie in wait to make an escape, and an adult loaded down with groceries or a kid rushing off to the playground can accidentally provide the necessary opening. Even if you live in an apartment or condo, a collar and tag may make sense. If your cat escapes into a hallway or stairwell, you want the person who finds it to call you, rather than the building manager.

Note that the collar should always be of the type (now available at pet stores everywhere) that contains at least an element of elastic so that the cat can wiggle out of it if, for example, the collar gets caught on a branch while the cat is climbing a tree, or on a nail while the cat is scaling a fence.

A cat door, which basically consists of a small flap covering an opening in your garage or some inconspicuous area of your house, can be a handy way of giving your cat the opportunity to come and go as it pleases. Available at pet stores and hardware stores everywhere, cat flaps can be of the type that opens either way, allowing the cat to both enter and exit, or the type that allows the cat only to enter. The latter might be useful if, for example, you'd like to permit your cat to return from its evening romp without having to awaken you by howling outside your bedroom, but you'd like to keep it in once it's back.

Note that a lock of some sort is useful in case unwanted visitors, feline or otherwise, discover the door.

Some cats take to cat doors instantly. Others require a bit of instruction, usually as little as holding the door open for them and placing a cat treat on the opposite side.

Perhaps the single greatest complaint about cats as pets is their tendency to scratch the furniture. And somehow, to add insult to injury, cats seem to zero in on the most expensive items.

Cats claw things, because (a) it feels good, (b) it keeps their nails in good condition, and (c) it leaves their mark, sort of like a flag posted in the dirt. (A cat's "mark" consists of paw sweat, which other cats can quickly

identify, as well as scratches.)
If provided with ample, suitably
textured scratching posts located
in adequately central locations—
cats want to leave their mark
prominently—a cat can often be
persuaded to leave the furniture
alone. The chances of attaining
this sort of behavioral modifica-
tion are best if coaching of the cat
occurs early and often. Specifically, any time you see your cat
(better yet, your kitten)
scratching the furni-
ture, grab it firmly,
plop it down in front
of the scratching
post, and physi-

cally rub its claws along the post to demonstrate the appealing texture.

Note that allowing a cat outdoors, where there are typically many socially acceptable scratching opportunities (trees), also reduces its tendency to scratch furniture.

Some cats seem incapable of giving up scratching the furniture, perhaps because their training commenced too late, perhaps because they're just hardheaded. Whatever the reason, the owner of such a cat is presented with a troubling dilemma: to declaw or not to declaw.

Supporters of declawing (as an option, when all other approaches have failed) contend that this relatively "minor" surgery—only the front two paws are ever declawed—can literally save the cat's life, because many cat owners would otherwise give the cat to the local humane society or the like, where it could end up being destroyed.

Opponents of declawing characterize the operation as "major"—it involves general anesthesia and a stay at the hospital—and as nothing short of mutilation, in the form of severing the cat's last "knuckles." They point out that it removes the cat's primary means of defense, in that a declawed cat can neither fight nor climb. In England, the procedure is illegal except when deemed medically necessary.

As with other debates over medical and moral issues, including many involving humans, the outcome in any given case seems more likely to be a matter of the heart than the head.

Maintaining strong, healthy

teeth is a challenge in cats, especially those that live on soft canned food. Cats in the wild clean their teeth by chomping on the tough skin, gristle, and bones of their prey, but domestic cats have to rely on dry food and regular dental checkups. Tartar accumulation is a particular problem. It can lead to painful inflammation of the gums and worse, ultimately causing loss of teeth. Not every cat will tolerate the otherwise highly beneficial weekly treatment with salt and water (rubbed on with a piece of cotton, or even a child's toothbrush) that can remove

tartar, so annual (or more frequent) monitoring and cleaning
by a professional is genuinely
necessary.

Cats spend a huge amount of
time grooming themselves, primarily with their tongues,
though their teeth and forepaws
also play a role. This is not only
natural, but desirable. Such
grooming cleans the fur, stimu-
lates blood circulation, and
even tones muscle.

There is also a nutritional as-
pect to grooming. Sunlight en-
ables the fur to produce vitamin
D, which the cat ingests in the

course of grooming. Finally, saliva on the fur performs essentially the same cooling function as sweat on human skin, cooling it via the evaporation process. Hence the increased grooming one can observe in warm weather or following periods of heavy activity.

If your cat should lose its interest in grooming, consider taking it in for a checkup. Physical illness, ranging from a mild bug to a serious disease, may be the explanation. Depression is also a possibility. Few veterinarians doubt that cats grieve the loss of a companion, whether feline or human. A depressed cat may require medication, but gentle, abundant care and nursing will in most instances remedy the problem.

Cats are as capable of developing eye trouble as humans. The greatest danger is not blindness, but foreign objects in the eye. If your cat is keeping one eye closed or pawing at it, or if you observe discharge from the eye, you should act promptly. First, hold the cat so as to prevent it from pawing the eye. Then, holding the cat's body firmly, and raising part of the eyelid, examine the eye. If you observe a superficial scratch or speck of sand or something similar, you may be able to ease the pain and remove the object by flooding the eye with a liquid such as tea. If you observe blood, or if the foreign object is in any way penetrating the surface of the eye, consult a vet immediately.

Cats love cozy, secure places, many of which may strike humans as hideaways. Although cats do enjoy curling up in small boxes, in dark corners of closets, and in similar spots, they aren't really hiding and will typically emerge after several hours for food, to use the litter box, or to enjoy a bit of companionship, feline or human.

On the other hand, a cat that is seriously ill may go into true hiding, not (as the myth goes) because it wishes to die alone, but because it senses when its diminished strength renders it most vulnerable to predators, and its natural self-preservation instinct leads it to seek out places where predators can't find it. The problem, of course, is that hiding may cost it the care of someone who could in fact save it. If your cat appears to be seeking a genuinely remote, unfindable hideaway, examine it closely for signs of illness.

Not many cats live beyond the age of twenty, and one that survives to the age of seventeen is doing well. As with humans, cats change as they grow older. Their hearing and eyesight decline, their bowels may become sluggish, their livers and kidneys may fail, and their eating habits may change.

The general rule in caring for an older cat is to be alert, noting any changes in its appearance or habits, and to respond appropriately. If your cat's hearing or eyesight appears to be failing, for example, you'll need to start keeping it inside. The danger from cars, dogs, or other cats is just too great. And you'll need to make sure its feeding bowls and litter box aren't moved.

Another age-related problem: If your cat shows signs of constipation, you may need to add mineral oil or oily fish to its diet. Try to clean the cat's teeth of

tartar more frequently now (as often as twice a week), and take it in for a checkup two or three times annually, as your vet recommends.

If your cat seems hard of hearing, the first thing to check is the color of your cat's coat and eyes. There is a genetic link between white coats, blue eyes, and deafness, especially among Persian cats, which for years were bred to achieve the bluest possible eyes, with a high incidence of deafness occurring incidentally. Many cats with one blue eye will be deaf (or partially deaf) in the ear on the same side. Hearing is, of course, less important for an indoor cat than an outdoor one, and many deaf cats develop such superb compensating senses that you may never notice the problem.

Still, it's worth getting a vet to look into it, though not urgently. Meanwhile, check for such things as buildup of wax in the ear, discharge or other signs of irritation in the ear, the cat holding its head to one side (which might indicate an infection in the ear), and anything else unusual.

A shorthaired cat that is normal and healthy can and usually will perform all the grooming (which generally means licking) that is necessary for the health and appearance of its fur and skin. Longhaired cats, on the other hand, absolutely require human help. A single day without brushing a longhaired cat can cause the hair to become matted, especially on the cat's stomach and inner legs, and the resulting tangles can generally be removed only by shaving the area.

Pedigreed (purebred) cats have distinctive traits, in terms of personality types and other features. To take just one example, Persian cats are comparatively quiet, and Siamese cats are comparatively noisy (and demanding). The benefit of this is that with a pedigreed cat, you know what you're getting, and you can choose accordingly. The downside is that pedigreed cats tend to have a higher incidence of certain types of diseases—the result of generations of inbreeding. Mixed breeds, in contrast, are relatively healthy and hardy, and they often have more relaxed dispositions. A mongrel kitten may be a bit of an uncertain commodity, but it could well prove to be a happier, healthier pet.

Sometimes a cat will go well beyond normal grooming and lick some area of its body (often its abdomen) entirely bald. There are several possible explanations for such behavior. First, check for fleas or other external parasites. If you find nothing, the problem may have psychological origins. Specifically, some change in the cat's world may have made it anxious or worried, and it may be responding just as humans often do in comparable situations—namely, with compulsive (excessive) levels of a type of conduct from which it is used to deriving comfort and a sense of order in its universe.

Have you just moved? Have you just had a baby? It would be enough if you were simply *preparing* for one of these things. A cat is a highly sensitive creature, and this applies not only to its sense of smell and hearing. Even in the early stages of a human owner's pregnancy, a cat just knows something dramatic is about to happen.

If the prospect of a new baby (or some other change) is genuinely diminishing your level of interest in the cat, the kindest course might be to find it a new home. Alternatively, give it some extra care and cuddling. Over time, your reassurances will likely ease the anxiety, and the cat will cut back on its grooming to normal, healthy levels.

Don't feed your cat aspirin. It's fine for humans and dogs, but it can be toxic, even lethal, for cats, whose bodies aren't equipped to break it down in the same way. If your cat is hobbling or otherwise acting in such a way as to make you suspect arthritis (which is conceivable but statistically far less likely

than in humans or dogs), a tiny amount of aspirin—say, a third of a standard tablet, administered every fourth day—might do some good. But your best bet is to consult a veterinarian.

Contrary to persistent myth, cats do not present a terrible threat to pregnant women. To be sure, a cat or any other animal that has contracted rabies is dangerous, but a rabid creature is a threat to everyone, not just to pregnant women. You can and should protect against that by having your cat vaccinated against rabies.

The one cat-related disease that is an appropriate subject of concern among pregnant women is toxoplasmosis, which can cause birth defects or miscarriage. Note, however, that cats themselves can acquire the internal parasite that causes this disease only by consuming live (or recently deceased) prey, and humans can contract it only by handling cat feces. Thus, if your cat consumes only commercially prepared food, there is no cause for concern, and the same is true if the pregnant woman doesn't clean the kitty litter. If you are in doubt as to what your cat might have consumed, either because you allow it outdoors or because it chases the occasional indoor mouse, reliable tests for toxoplasmosis are available, and the cat that tests positive can be treated. Thus, if someone in your household is pregnant, your cat certainly need not be given away or destroyed out of concern for the fetus.

All cats should be vaccinated against the major infectious diseases. If you're about to acquire a kitten, make sure it has been vaccinated, preferably at least one week before you take it. If you're getting an adult cat, check its records to confirm that it received all appropriate vaccinations as a kitten and regular booster shots thereafter.

The first vaccinations—for *feline influenza* ("cat flu"), *feline enteritis,* and *feline leukemia*—should come at eight or nine weeks after birth. The second vaccinations (for the same diseases) should come three or four weeks later. Annual boosters should be given thereafter.

Vaccinations against rabies also are available, advisable, and often they are required by law.

You may at some point observe your cat engaging in the bizarre and somewhat comical-looking act of "scooting." Starting from a seated position, the cat will drag its rump across the floor (or sofa or bed), almost invariably leaving a visible fecal trail ranging in length from a few inches to a few feet. It is not unreasonable to suspect that your fastidious cat is, in effect, "wiping" his bottom.

Actually, however, your cat is trying to relieve itself of the considerable discomfort that accompanies impacted (or possibly infected) anal glands. These are two small sacs on either side of the anus that discharge a bad-smelling (to humans) fluid each time the cat defecates. For any of various reasons, the cat may find itself unable to discharge this fluid in the normal way. The resulting impaction may lead to infection, parasite infestation, and—almost certainly—pain.

The bad news is that this problem is unlikely to go away on its own. The cat's scooting may relieve the itching for a while, but you're almost certain to see it, with similarly displeasing results, again. The good news is that vets can quickly, easily, and inexpensively empty (or "express") the glands simply by squeezing them with their fingers, and there's no real pain involved for the cat.

Feline first aid is a challenge, to say the least, for the average nonveterinarian. This is why, in the event of an emergency, your best bet is to call a vet right away. (Better yet, have someone else call the vet, while you tend to the cat.) Keep the telephone number of your vet and the local around-the-clock animal hospital in a convenient place near the phone.

Meanwhile:
- If your cat has stopped breathing, open its mouth, check for obstacles to breathing, and use your fingers to remove anything you see. You could even try swinging the cat around by its hind legs.
- If your cat gets burned, apply cold water or ice to the injured area. If chemicals are involved, wash the site thoroughly, using huge amounts of water.

- If your cat is bleeding, try to stop the flow by applying pressure.
- If your cat has suffered a blow and is unconscious or very weak, keep it horizontal. Do not lift its head, lest blood, vomit, or saliva flow back and block its airway.
- If your cat has consumed poison, the proper response depends on the particular type of poison. For example, sometimes you should feed the cat an emetic, and sometimes you shouldn't. In any event, keep a sample of whatever the cat has consumed, so the

vet can determine the precise nature of the poison. If the cat has consumed the poison by licking it off its fur, prevent the cat from further licking, perhaps by wrapping its body in a blanket, with only the cat's head sticking out.

THE EVOLUTION OF THE CAT

Cats are mammals—which means, among other things, that they produce living offspring (rather than eggs that hatch into offspring), they feed their young with milk from the female mammary glands, their bodies are substantially covered with hair, and their body temperature is self-regulating.

The carnivorous (meat-eating) mammals from which modern-day cats evolved prowled the earth some 40 million to 45 million years ago. Fossils showing a strong resemblance to today's cat date back approximately 12 million years, and animals essentially the same as the creatures we would readily recognize as cats made their first appearance between 3 and 5 million years ago, in the Early Pliocene epoch. While other mammals' ancestors of that era would hardly be recognizable today, cats seem to have changed comparatively little for several million years.

More than a few members of the cat family have passed into extinction over the millennia. At least 13,000 years have passed since the saber-toothed tiger, which once prowled virtually everywhere, ceased walking the earth. Other now-extinct cats include the giant tiger of Asia and the cave lion of Europe, both of which may have vanished even earlier than the saber-toothed tiger. More re-

cent breeds that have met ex-
tinction include the Mexican
Hairless, which existed only in
Mexico in the late 1800s.

One breed that almost died
out but has since returned to
abundance is the Abyssinian
(which strongly re-
sembles the sacred cats
of ancient Egypt but is
not believed to be di-
rectly related). The
Abyssinian found itself
on the brink of extinc-
tion during World War
II, when meat, a critical
component of its diet,
was in perilously short supply.

Although some disagreement among taxonomists persists, the cat family ("Felidae") is generally considered to include three genuses (in the traditional scheme of zoological classifications: phylum, class, order, family, genus, species, and variety). These genuses are: (1) *Panthera*, which includes the big cats, such as lions, whose bones in the mouth area are configured in such a way that they are able to roar; (2) *Felis*, the smaller cats, whose bone structure does not permit them to roar; and (3) *Acinonyx*, which includes only the cheetah, distinguished by several features, including its relatively small canines, its wide nasal apertures, and the fact that its claws are not fully retractable.

Some forty species of cat exist today. The species with the greatest variety is the domestic house cat, which has thrived and multiplied in diverse forms largely as a result of the aid of humans. Before humans entered the picture, the colors and patterns of cats' coats reflected their environment, evolving primarily so as to camouflage them from both their predators and their prey. Controlled breeding by humans, however, has yielded physical variety unrelated to environmental considerations.

Cats now live on every continent except Antarctica. By a few million years ago, cats had spread throughout most of the globe on their own, but humans introduced them to a number of new places, including Australia. Human introduction of cats into new environments has sometimes produced troubling consequences. For example, humans introduced felines to the

Galápagos Islands, in the Pacific Ocean off the coast of Ecuador; the result was disastous for a number of indigenous creatures that until then had never required the need for defense against this type of predator.

Today, some 34 percent of the homes in the United States have at least one cat, and Americans own almost 70 million cats over-

all. (There are more dog households in the United States— about 36 percent—but fewer dogs overall: about 58 million.)

The earliest instances of feline domestication are difficult to pinpoint, but it has been authenticated as having occurred at least by 1500 B.C. (and probably took place a good bit earlier than that). The cat was declared sacred during the fifth and sixth Egyptian dynasties (approximately 2500 B.C. to approximately 2100 B.C.), although kitties may not have been actually scratching furniture and eating houseplants quite that early!

Art and literature suggest that cats were prowling human abodes in Greece and China as early as the fifth century B.C., and Sanskrit records speak of cats in India around the first century B.C. On the other hand, Arabia and Japan may have had to wait until A.D. 600 for feline domestication. And in Britain, the earliest records of domestic cats involve a Welsh prince who passed feline protection legislation in the tenth century A.D.

Cats, especially black ones, have

long been associated with religion and the occult. Ancient Egyptians worshipped a cat-headed goddess named Bast, and archeological digs in Egypt have turned up numerous cat mummies. (These digs have also turned up mouse mummies, presumably to serve in the hereafter as food or perhaps entertainment for the cats.)

Cats have played similarly sig-

nificant roles in religions of Scandinavia and Asia. And the history of the English-speaking countries, certainly including the United States, is rife with references to cats as major players in sorcery and witchcraft.

In at least one respect, feline evolution has paralleled that of camels and giraffes more than, for example, dogs. Specifically, cats run not by moving both front legs and then both rear legs, the way a dog (or horse) does, but by

moving both the front leg and rear leg on one side, and then the front leg and rear leg on the other side. No other animals except the camel and the giraffe run in this manner.

Scientists speculate that Egyptians first domesticated the cat upon recognizing the feline talent for catching and destroying grain-eating rodents. Necessary precursors of that development, however, were the more fundamental shifts in human existence involving the development of agriculture and the trend toward urbanization, which together generated not only food surpluses, but also food waste—in sufficient quantity to attract and support otherwise feral, solitary, free-roving cats.

These cats were scavengers, and their move into proximity to—and cohabitation with—humans proved a spectacularly successful evolutionary development. The key to evolutionary survival is a capacity for adaptation, and by allowing themselves to be domesticated, cats adapted magnificently to one of the greatest changes imaginable, namely, the spread of human beings across the globe.

Saber-toothed tigers were the first "cats" to propagate and survive in large numbers on this planet. They became established some 34 million years ago (as did various other mammals, largely in response to the cooling of Earth's climate). Their strikingly elongated upper teeth, which surely hindered the basic process of eating, would seem to have made them unlikely candidates for an evolutionary success story, but in fact they survived substantially longer than modern cats have been around (or, for that matter, humans). Their demise coincided with the extinction of the

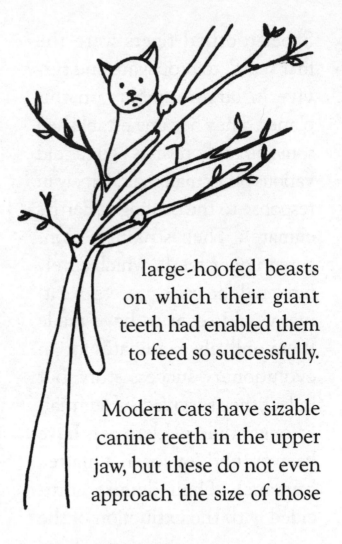

large-hoofed beasts on which their giant teeth had enabled them to feed so successfully.

Modern cats have sizable canine teeth in the upper jaw, but these do not even approach the size of those of the now extinct saber-toothed cats. On the other hand, modern cats also have sizable (almost as large) canines in the lower jaw. Together, these upper and lower canines approximate the length of the daggers of the upper jaw in their ancestors.

The cheetah, which is the world's fastest land animal (clocked at speeds approaching seventy miles per hour), is at the opposite end of the spectrum from the saber-toothed cats, in that it has proportionally the smallest canine teeth of any cat. On the other hand, it has large nasal openings that permit the rapid air intake necessary for high-speed chase, and it possesses other unique structural and physiological features that contribute to the same end. Thus, while the cheetah may not have evolved with the fierce weaponry of the saber-tooths, evolution has endowed it with other assets such that, in a one-on-one footrace for survival (loser gets eaten), the cheetah usually prevails.

Cats present special challenges for taxonomists, scientists who specialize in the classification of living creatures. For one thing, the cheetah occupies an entire genus all by itself. Also odd is the puma, which by any calculation in inches or centimeters should rank as at least a mid-size cat, but is generally called a "small" cat because of minute features of certain bones in its throat. Then there are the ocelot and margay, which are placed in the subgenus *Leopardus*, because they have only thirty-six chromosomes, rather than thirty-eight, like most cats, including domestic house cats. (Humans have forty-six.) Disagreements regarding various aspects of cat taxonomy persist to this day.

Although a number of cats such as the saber-toothed tiger passed into extinction without "help" from humans, others have been forever lost or are on the verge of being lost as a direct result of human causes. Consider, for example, the different forms of tiger. The Balinese tiger vanished from the earth in 1937. The Javanese tiger followed soon after, as did the Caspian tiger. Guns, poison, and deforestation have reduced the population of tigers in Asia by

95 percent in the space of less than one human life span.

A similar fate has befallen various types of lions. What was believed to be the last southern Cape lion was killed by hunters in 1865, and the Barbary lion passed out of existence in 1922.

Particularly at risk among the

world's remaining cats are those like the tiger and jaguar, which require not only large spaces in which to hunt, but large spaces of a specific type (for example, forests). (This requirement is in contrast to leopards, for example, which are able to survive in somewhat more diverse environments.)

On average, mixed-breed cats live substantially longer than purebred cats. The former are simply genetically hardier. As a result of that fact alone, 90 percent of all domestic cats are mixed breed, notwithstanding the opposite impression one might get at cat shows and the like.

Only in a few geographically isolated areas have purebred cats developed naturally. The Japanese Bobtail in Japan, for example, or the Angora in Anatolia, or the Siamese in Thailand (once Siam)—all developed without dilution by other breeds.

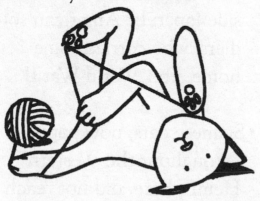

The role of humans in the development and geographic dissemination of diverse breeds is hard to overstate. Among numerous individual examples:

- The Japanese Bobtail, a cat distinguished by its short curled tail (typically four or five inches in the adult), was introduced to the world outside Japan by American soldiers, who carried some home after World War II.

- Siamese cats, now popular throughout the Western Hemisphere, did not reach

England until the late 1800s, as gifts from the king of Siam to the British consul-general in Bangkok.

• The first Himalayan cat was born at Harvard Medical School in 1935, the result of deliberate crossing of several breeds, including the Persian and Siamese.

Evolution, with or without help from man, has yielded notable differences in the personalities and temperaments of various breeds of cats, as well as differences in their color and other physical features. For example:

- The Siamese cat is one of the few that can be trained to walk on a leash like a dog.

- The Turkish Van cat likes to swim.

- The Maine Coon cat habitually sleeps in odd positions in odd places.

FAMOUS CAT OWNERS, PAST AND PRESENT

ARTISTIC CATS

Pierre Auguste Renoir

Renoir loved his three sons and had a fascination with cats. Both his sons and various cats were portrayed in many of his paintings. In one of them, *Child with Cat (Miss Julie Manet)*, a beautiful, wistful young girl holds a cat that is so perfectly content it appears to be smiling.

CATS OF THE BIG AND LITTLE SCREENS

Christina Applegate

Christina Applegate is the actress who portrayed Kelly, the ditzy blond daughter of Al and Peg Bundy, on *Married with Children*. Natasha and Jesse are her two black cats.

Downtown Julie Brown

This former MTV-VJ and current host of E! channel's *The Gossip Show* owns two cats. They were originally named Rum and Coke, but Brown's neighbors gave her funny looks whenever she'd call out the back door "Coke! Coke!". To avoid trouble, she renamed the cats Vodka and Tonic.

Regis Philbin

The star of *Live! with Regis and Kathie Lee* owns a Persian cat.

The Simpsons

Even a cartoon family needs pets! The Simpson's first cat, Snowball, never appeared "on-screen." The poor kitty was killed in a car accident and replaced by Snowball 2. Unlike the Simpsons' dog, Santa's Little Helper, Snowball 2 is a minor cartoon character.

Martha Stewart

Stewart, unlike a cat, is said to need only four hours of sleep a day. She is, however, the proud owner of six cats, two of whom are named Teeny and Weeny.

Patrick Stewart

Since leaving *Star Trek: the Next Generation*, Stewart has been taking on some dastardly roles. In a *Today Show* interview, he said of his bad-guy role in the film *Conspiracy Theory*, "I think

I'm going to have to take out ads in the trades when this movie opens. You know, to explain that I have a cat and I'm nice to her."

Jonathan Taylor Thomas

This sixteen-year-old actor appears weekly in the popular sitcom *Home Improvement*. He has also played lead roles in the films *Huck and Tom* and *Wild America,* and is a major animal lover who won't eat meat or use products that have been tested on animals. In 1994, he did the voice-over of the young lion destined to be king in *The Lion*

King. Is it any wonder that he has a cat named Simba? Samantha, a Himalayan who is Simba's mom, is his other kitty.

Vanna White

As hostess of the game show *Wheel of Fortune*, Vanna White has been destined to turn heads and letters. Vanna often speaks lovingly of her two cats on the show.

LITERARY CATS

Dr. Samuel Johnson

The son of a bookseller, Johnson

grew up to become the most famous writer in eighteenth-century England. He had a pet cat named Hodge and fed him extravagant treats like oysters. He didn't ask the servants to run this errand because he feared it would make them dislike the cat.

Lewis Carroll

Cat-lover Carroll created the Cheshire Cat, who would slowly fade away and leave only his smile.

Charles Dickens

When Dickens's cat gave birth

to a litter, the author allowed only one to remain in his house with the mother. The kitten was known thereafter as the Master's Cat, and it would snuff out Dickens's reading candle to capture his attention.

Alexandre Dumas

The author of *The Three Musketeers* and *The Count of Monte Cristo* had an unusual cat named Mysouff. Every day, Mysouff would accompany Dumas to his office and then walk back home. At the end of a long day, the cat would scratch on the door to be let out so he

could meet Dumas at his office and accompany him home. This behavior isn't all that unusual; cats seem to have an internal clock that senses what time it is. They always know when it's time to be fed, don't they? What made Mysouff so unique was his extrasensory perception. When Dumas had to work late, the cat seemed to know it, and he wouldn't ask to be let out at the normal time.

Ernest Hemingway

This American writer owned about thirty cats, including some six-toed polydactyls. Descendants of these cats still live in Hemingway's old home at Key West, Florida.

Victor Hugo

Many entries in Hugo's diary refer to his pet cats.

Edgar Allan Poe

Poe often used cats as sinister figures in his stories, such as "The Black Cat." Yet Poe loved cats, and that particular story had been written with his pet Catarina in mind. Over the years, he had many cats. The winter of 1846–1847 was one of Poe's particularly destitute times; he and his wife, Virginia, had no food, no fuel, and no money. One visitor found Virginia, dying from tuberculosis, with only her husband's overcoat and one large tortoiseshell cat to warm her.

Sir Walter Scott

Hinse was the name of Scott's vicious tomcat. He would terrorize Scott's dogs to the point of distraction and often swatted them away to seize their meals. Is it any wonder that he finally met his death at the teeth of a dog?

Harriet Beecher Stowe

The author of *Uncle Tom's Cabin* befriended a cat she named Calvin when he showed up on her doorstep one day. A true writer's cat, Calvin would often sit upon Stowe's shoulder as she worked.

Carl Van Vetchen

Carl Van Vetchen, the American novelist who wrote *Peter Whiffle* and *Spider Boy*, owned a cat named Ariel. Ariel, an orange Persian, had an uncharacteristic love of water. She loved to sit under a running tap or leap into the author's bath with him. Ariel was also a retriever and a hider, and would stash small items under the rug.

Horace Walpole

Horace Walpole, the English

writer considered to have established the Gothic genre with *The Castle of Otranto*, had a cat named Selima. When Selima

drowned in a goldfish bowl, Walpole's companion, Thomas Gray, wrote a poem entitled "On the Death of a Favorite Cat Drowned in a Tub of Goldfish."

MUSICAL CATS

Mark Lindsay

The former lead singer of the 1960s group, Paul Revere and the Raiders, and his wife, Deb, travel between two homes— one in Idaho and one in Maui. Their cat, Sparky, is always with them.

Ric Ocasek

Singer-songwriter Ocasek, for- mer member of the band the Cars, leaves his television on twenty-four hours a day for his cats because he feels "they like

the voices and the action. They all hang out in the kitchen with the TV."

Domenico Scarlatti

The Italian composer owned a cat named Pulcinella, who would often leap onto the keys of his harpsichord. Might she have helped him write his famous "The Cat's Fugue"?

Albert Schweitzer

Sizi lived with Nobel Prize winner, musician, and medical missionary Schweitzer at his clinic in Africa. It was obvious to visitors that Schweitzer had deep affection for the cat because he was often seen catering to her every need.

POETIC CATS

Matthew Arnold

Victorian poet Arnold had a canary named Matthias and a Persian cat, Atossa. When the cat was very old, he would sit in front of the canary's cage for hours, never moving, realizing his bird-catching days were at an end. Arnold captured the scene and the essence of his old cat in one of his poems:

Cruel, but composed and bland,
Dumb, inscrutable and grand,
So Tiberius might have sat,
Had Tiberius been a cat.

Edward Lear

Victorian artist and humorist Lear, known for making the limerick famous, wrote:

The Owl and the Pussy-cat
went to sea
    In a beautiful pea green boat,
    They took some honey, and
plenty of money,
    Wrapped up in a five pound
note.
    Lear's beloved cat, Foss, wasn't
known for his beauty. He had a
wide body, a strange expression,
and a short tail. His tail was the
victim of one of Lear's servants,

who believed that by chopping off the cat's tail, he could prevent the cat from wandering. Although the cat came away tail-impaired, Lear adored him, and when Foss died, he received a full burial in Lear's Italian garden.

Pierre Loti

Pierre Loti was the pseudonym of Louis-Marie-Julien Viaud, a French naval officer, travel writer, and novelist. In 1906, the painter Henri Rousseau did a portrait of Loti that may have been in honor of Loti's acceptance into the Academie Française. Loti, a great cat lover who often wrote of his pets, is portrayed wearing a fez and standing behind a tabby.

Dorothy L. Sayers

The creator of Lord Peter Wimsey also wrote poems. Two of them, "For Timothy" and "War Cat," were written for her pet cat, Timothy.

W. B. Yeats

Yeats was a cat lover and owner. He studied the movements of cats' pupils and likened them to the waxing and waning of the moon in his poem about the black cat Minnaloushe:

Does Minnaloushe know that his pupils
Will pass from change to change,
And that from round to crescent
From crescent to round they range?

POLITICAL CATS

Ron Brown

Alma, the wife of the late secretary of commerce Ron Brown, was once told she could not board a plane with her cat; there wasn't enough room.

Brown canceled their flight—
although he was running late—
and booked a later flight so that
he, his wife, *and* the cat could all
travel together.

Sir Winston Churchill

Sir Winston loved his cat so

much that he commissioned a portrait of the orange tabby. In 1953, a stray black kitten showed up at 10 Downing Street and was also adopted by the prime minister. Since Churchill had just delivered a powerful speech at Margate that had been well received, he named the cat Margate.

Charles de Gaulle

This French general once owned a Chartreux cat, known for its dense, blue-colored fur and its orange eyes.

The Downing Street Cat

A longhaired black-and-white stray appeared at the door of Number 10 Downing Street one day to be adopted by Margaret Thatcher. "Humphrey" became the official mouser of the prime minister's quarters. He stayed on through the term of Prime Minister John Major and into the term of Prime Minister Tony Blair.

Early in Blair's term, rumors arose that all was not bliss between the new Downing Street family and Humphrey. To assure everyone that everything was just peachy at home, Mrs. Blair—a known feline hater—was forced to sit for a photograph with the cat to prove that there was no enmity between the new residents and the resident cat.

Mysteriously, in late 1997, Humphrey disappeared. The Blairs told the press that the cat was old and infirm, but the public wasn't buying the story. The government released photographs of Humphrey on his sickbed, but some complained that they weren't photos of the same cat.

The Third Earl of Southampton

During the reign of Elizabeth I, the earl was imprisoned in the Tower of London. His cat, Trixie, traveled across London all by herself and down the chimney to her master's cell. She stayed with him until his release two years later.

Harold Wilson

Nemo, the pet of Prime Minister Wilson and his wife, would accompany his owners on their annual vacation to the Scilly Islands, a group of small islands off the coast of England. This was as far as the Wilsons would travel; they wanted to avoid quarantining their cat, which would have been necessary had they left England.

RELIGIOUS CATS

Mohammed

One day, when Mohammed was called to prayer, he found his cat, Muezza, asleep on the sleeve of his robe. Mohammed cut off the sleeve rather than disturb the feline. When Mohammed returned, the cat awakened and bowed in thanks to his master. Mohammed stroked Muezza three times, and assured him a permanent place in Islamic paradise.

Pope Leo XII

Micetto was a black-striped, grayish-red cat born in the Vatican. He was frequently seen nestling among the folds of the Pope Leo's robe.

Cardinal Richelieu

Richelieu served as the chief minister of state to Louis XIII from 1624 to 1642, and he was known for his affection for cats. He was particularly fond of Lucifer, a black Angora.

SCIENTIFIC CAT

Sir Isaac Newton

Sir Isaac had so many cats that he invented the swinging cat door for their—and undoubtedly his own!—convenience.

WHITE HOUSE CATS

George Washington

The Washington cats never

lived in the White House, since it wasn't ready for occupants while George was still in office. However, Martha may have been the first American to have Newton's ingenious cat door installed, at Mount Vernon.

Abraham Lincoln

Lincoln had a tender heart for cats. Once, when Lincoln was

visiting Ulysses S. Grant's headquarters, he came upon three kittens wandering aimlessly. Lincoln was told that their mother had been killed. He picked them all up, lovingly petted them, then advised a high-ranking member of Grant's staff, "Colonel, I hope you will see that these poor, little, motherless waifs are given plenty of milk and treated kindly."

Mrs. Rutherford B. Hayes

Upon coming to the White House, Mrs. Hayes left her cats in her home state of Ohio. She felt they would be happier and better cared for there, but she missed them terribly. Eventually news of her sadness reached the press and was noticed by the U.S. consul in Bangkok, David Sickels. He had been hoping to gain favor for Siam with the new president and thought the gift of a Siamese kitten to Mrs. Hayes would be a good way to get noticed. After all, it would be the first Siamese kitten in America.

The Siamese breed was considered royal in Siam and had not been exported, although sailors had snuck out a few. Sickels got permission from the king to make his gift and chose the female kitten himself. Although Sickels named the kitten Miss Pussy, Lucy Hayes renamed her Siam.

William McKinley

William McKinley and his wife, Ida, were owners of the first longhaired cat in the White House, an Angora. Known only as "Ida's Cat," she became "Ida's Mamma Cat" after she had a litter of kittens.

Theodore Roosevelt

Roosevelt owned two cats— Tom Quartz and Slippers, who

moved into the White House in 1901. The president is said to have loved them very much. With Tom Quartz, he played a kind of tag that involved Tom's nipping at the president's trousers. The cat is said to have carried the game a bit too far when he nipped at the trousers of a visiting dignitary and would not let go.

Slippers was a gray tabby with six toes on his front paws. The tips of all his paws were white, which is how he got his name. Once while the cat was sleeping in the White House hallway, Roosevelt led distinguished guests around him, rather than disturb his rest. After seating his guests comfortably in the East Room, Roosevelt went back to scoop up the cat. He returned to the East Room and sat Slippers on his wife's lap, where he could be petted and admired.

Woodrow Wilson

Wilson owned a white cat with golden eyes.

Calvin Coolidge

Coolidge was the owner of three felines—Blackie, Tiger, and Bounder. But Coolidge wasn't only a cat owner. He owned an entire menagerie, including a pigmy hippo, a bear, and a bobcat.

Caroline Kennedy

Tom Kitten, the pet of President John F. Kennedy's daughter Caroline, became a White House cat in 1960. When Tom died in 1962, he was lovingly remembered in a newspaper obituary. But Tom Kitten wasn't the most famous Kennedy pet. It was Caroline's dog, Pushinka, a gift from Nikita Khrushchev. Pushinka was suspected by some of being a Russian spy.

Susan Ford

Chan, the Siamese cat of President Gerald Ford's daughter, Susan, took up White House residence in 1974. He padded the White House halls for two years, until the next Siamese came along.

Amy Carter

In 1977, Amy Carter's Siamese, Misty Malarky Ying Yang, replaced Chan and remained in the White House for four years.

Chelsea Clinton

The present First Cat is a black-and-white, mixed-breed stray that was adopted by the current First Daughter, Chelsea Clinton. Socks, the lucky feline, is named for the white at the end of his four paws. He is the first First Cat to have been reelected in the twentieth century, and the first cat to reside in the White

House since Amy Carter's Misty
Malarky Ying Yang left in 1981.
Socks's diary, *Socks Goes to Washington*, was published in 1993,

and he has his own fan club and a home page on the World Wide Web. At the click of a mouse, you can even hear him "meow."

SCARED SILLY: CAT SUPERSTITIONS FROM AROUND THE WORLD

BEST WISHES

Cats with only one eye are known as harbingers of luck. If, after encountering one, you spit on your thumb, jab it into the palm of your hand, and make a wish, no doubt the wish will come true.

WHITE IS BLACK

In some parts of England, white cats are considered bad luck.

BREATH ROBBERS

People once believed that cats might creep into nurseries to steal babies' breath. Nursemaids were ordered to stand constant watch over the little ones to protect them from the dreaded cat.

CATCHOO!

Some Italians believed that a cat sneeze meant good fortune for all who heard it. In other parts of the world, a cat sneeze on the morning of a wedding day meant the couple would have a happy marriage. On any other day, however, it signaled rain. If a cat sneezed three times in a row, some were convinced that everyone in the house would come down with a cold.

CATGUT DOESN'T REALLY COME FROM CATS' GUTS

Around A.D. 1300, saddle makers in Salle, Italy, realized that strands of sheep's intestines they'd been using to sew saddles made sweet musical tones when stretched and vibrated. A man named Erasmo, who later became St. Erasmo, found that these strands could also be used to make the strings for musical instruments.

The people of Salle developed an important industry out of string making, but kept their ingredient a secret to safeguard their corner on the market. So, whenever anyone asked what the strings were made from, they would reply, "catgut." Around that time, the killing of a cat was considered bad luck, and by lying, the string makers were able to protect their indus-

try; few others were willing to take the chance of killing cats.

CHASING LUCK

Never chase a black cat away or it will take the luck of your home with it. However, it is lucky to own a black cat or to meet one outdoors. Just never let it cross your path or you're in for a stretch of rocky road!

CURES FOR WHAT AILS YOU

You can cure a sty on the eye by moving a cat's tail downward over the eye and reciting the charm: "I poke thee. I don't poke thee. I poke the queff [the sty] that's under the eye. O qualyway, O qualyway." This procedure is also said to work well for warts and itching.

Applying dried cat skin to the face was thought to cure toothaches, and a whole cat boiled in oil was a seventeenth-century cure for wounds. If you wanted to relieve any other illness or one that wasn't remedied by these methods, it was considered best to throw the ailing person's bathwater onto the cat and to drive the animal from the house. Yet if a cat left home of its own accord, it was considered a portent of death.

In the southern portion of the United States, the broth from a boiled black cat has been said to be a cure for tuberculosis.

EXORCISM

The liver of a black cat was often included in the tools of exorcism.

THE WITCHING HOUR

Black cats aren't the only felines associated with witches. People have believed that witches could transfer their spirit into any cat. A witch could only perform this ritual transfer nine times, though, because a cat only had nine lives. And when a witch was killed, the witch's cat was often murdered with her.

FELINE
TIMEPIECES

In New England, cats were once used to tell the time: It was believed that the pupils of their eyes contracted at low tide and dilated at high tide.

KEEPING YOUR LUCK

Cats were sometimes sealed inside the walls of houses and other buildings during the Middle

Ages to guarantee the structure's good luck. In parts of England, it was standard practice to abandon the family cat after a spell of hard times. To avoid bad luck in school, some English children will spit or turn around in a circle and make the sign of the cross whenever they see a white cat on the way to school.

Through the ages, actors have considered cats lucky, but believe that kicking one would bring misery. In the southern United States, it was believed that kicking a cat would cause rheumatism, but if you drowned it, you would meet up with the devil. In Pennsylvania, however, it was believed that by boiling a black cat, you could keep the devil away.

KITTY SHIELDS

During the Persian invasions of Egypt in the sixth century B.C., Persian soldiers often captured and tied cats to their shields. It was impossible for the Egyptians, who worshiped cats, to kill or even harm them, thus

giving the Persians the upper hand in the battle.

CATS AND DEATH

Sick and dying cats were often put out of the house, out of fear that death would be carried through the feline to other members of the household.

Some Irish believed that if a

cat crossed your path in the moonlight, you would die—in an epidemic.

HOW TO COOK A CAT

On Easter Sunday and on Shrove Tuesday in England, cats were roasted to drive away evil spirits. And on the English holiday of Guy Fawkes Day, sacks of live cats were thrown into bonfires.

On St. John's Eve, a cat or two would be cooked over a fire while other domestic animals were driven through the smoke. The ashes of the poor cats were scooped up and retained as a magical powder.

SAILING CATS

Seamen believed that it was lucky to have a cat on board a ship. If the vessel needed wind, all the crew had to do was place a cat under a pot on deck. Throwing a cat overboard was to be avoided at all costs, as doing so could cause a storm, especially if the feline was all black. If a cat licked its fur in the wrong direction or scratched the legs of a table, a storm was also expected.

SECOND SIGHT

In the Scottish Highlands, during Taigheirin (a ritual from the Middle Ages in which cats were sacrificed and offered to the devil), black cats were burned alive in order to obtain the gift of second sight—clairvoyance. This practice continued until close to the end of the eighteenth century.

SOUL CARRIERS

In parts of West Africa, it is still believed that when people die, their souls pass out of their bodies and into the bodies of cats.

UNLUCKY MAY

Cats born in May were usually drowned, since they were thought to be poor mousers, capable of hunting only glow-worms and snakes. They were also thought to exhibit a melancholy disposition that was quite undesirable in a cat.

VAMPIRE MAKERS

It was once believed that if a cat encountered a human corpse, it would snatch the soul of the dead person, who would then become a vampire.

Another belief held that it

was bad luck for a cat to leap over a coffin, since it meant ill tidings for the deceased in the afterlife. The unsuspecting cat usually met an untimely death for its innocent behavior.

VICTIMS OF THE SPANISH INQUISITION

The Spanish Inquisition, which began in 1231, was a terrible time in cat history. Cats were considered representatives of the devil, and anyone known to harbor or aid a cat was punished by death. Cats were tortured and sometimes burned alive because it was believed that no torture was too severe for the devil.

WEATHER BAROMETERS

If a cat sits with its back to the fire, it can mean there will be frost or a storm. When a cat sleeps with all its paws tucked underneath its body, there will be cold weather.

If a cat scampers about wildly, there will be wind, but if it washes its ears, you'd better get your umbrella—it's definitely going to rain. And when Indonesians want it to rain, they just pour a little water over a cat's back.

SURFING THE PET NET: SOME CAT WEB SITES

COMPREHENSIVE SITES

Acme Pet Marketplace

http://www.acmepet.com/
feline/market/index.html

A whole page of click-through buttons awaits. Find information on everything from cat insurance to urns for your pets, and where and how to buy such items.

Cat Lovers Home Page at the Mining Company

http://catlovers.miningco.com/mbody.htm

"Greatest Cat" contests, clip art, and kitty postcards can be found on this site, along with a list of links, a bulletin board, a cat chatroom, and even a newsletter about cats to which you can subscribe.

The Cat Fanciers' Association

http://www.cfainc.org/

Learn about cat breeds, cat shows, and the latest cat news, hosted by the world's largest registry of pedigreed cats.

Waltham

http://www.waltham.com/pets/cats/c.htm

Hosted by the pet-food giant Waltham, this site offers extensive information on cats and cat care. You can learn how to choose a cat, how to train a cat, and even how to play with a cat. And if you like taking pictures of your darling, this site offers tips on cat photography.

JUST FOR FUN

Basic Rules for Cats Who Have a House to Run

http://geog.utoronto.ca/reynolds/pethumor/catrules.html

Cats have to learn how to control their humans, right? This guide provides plenty of

useful information for kitties—
and their owners!—who know
how to read.

Cat Dictionary

http://www.maths.qmw.ac.uk/~
lms/cats/catdic.html

Do you know what a "basket
case" is? It's a cat who sleeps in
a basket, of course. Or how
about an "alarm cat," as in "It is
4 A.M. and the alarm cat just
went off"? Wonder no more
about such terms. They're all
defined here at the click of a
mouse.

Feline Reactions to Bearded Men

http://www.improb.com/
airchives/cat.html

This site offers a study that tested the reactions of felines to men with and without beards. The conclusions are astounding and funny!

Library Cats Map

http://www2.thecia.net/users/
ironfrog/catsmap.html

Did you know that there are 257 known library cats—that is, cats who live or have lived in libraries—in the United States, past and present? This interactive map will tell you where to find them.

Map to Cat's Brain

http://www.ee.techpta.ac.za/cats/catbrain.html
Where is the "licking gland" in a cat's brain? How about the

"hatred of dogs" area or the "infatuation with people who hate cats" spot? At this hilarious site, these and other mysteries of the cat's brain are given a complete—and comic—evaluation.

MARKETPLACE

Cat Faeries Catalog

http://www.catfaeries.com/catalog1.html

This catalog of fine gifts and accessories sells everything uniquely "cat." Buy a cat-shaped backpack or grow your own indoor grass specially for your cat

pal who lives indoors or is suffering from the winter doldrums.

Kitty Korner

http://healthypaws.com/kitty.
html
    Here you will find lots of things
for a cat to "get into." Scratching
posts, electronic mice, and even
a kitty condo will entice the loving owner of the pampered cat.

Alley Cat Allies: Guidelines to Trap, Neuter, and Release

http://www.alleycat.org/ffn/tnr.html

If you're an activist and want to help control the feral cat population, this site offers information you will need to begin "managing" a feral cat colony.

Cats Belong Indoors

http://www.austinspca.com/catsindoor.html

In case you've been wonder-

ing, there are many good reasons why cats should remain indoors. This comprehensive list
covers the main points concerning this issue and will help you
to make an informed choice.

The Cat Consultant

http://www.angelfire.com/ar/
aruba1/cat.html

At this site, find answers to
common questions like "What
should I do when my cat has
runny eyes?" or "What if my cat
won't eat?" For a fee, you can
even consult an expert and
have your question answered
via e-mail.

Feline CRF Information Center

http://www.best.com/~lynxpt

Feline Chronic Renal Failure is a problem for many older cats. The answers to many questions relating to feline kidney disease are available at this site.

A Pet Owner's Guide to Common Small Animal Poisons

http://www.avma.org/pubhlth/poisgde.html

Get tips on how to avoid a cat disaster—here, you'll learn all about plants, drugs, household products, and miscellaneous items that are poisonous to your cat.

Adoptable Cats

http://www.access.digex.net/ ~rescue/CATS/cats.html

Here you can find many cats available for adoption. Some are months old, others are years old, while some are still newborns. All cats are described in detail and some even have pictures. Learn how to go about adopting the cat of your choice.

Cat Quilts

http://www.execpc.com/~judy-heim/catqlts.html

If you like to quilt and you like cats, this page presents many possibilities. There are plenty of pictures of cat quilts to view and information on how to obtain cat-quilt software to craft an "electronic quilt."

Names for Your Cat

http://expage.com/page/names-foryourcat

Anyone looking for the perfect name for a cat will find this categorized page very helpful.

WONDERFUL LINKS

Individual Cat Pages

http://pibweb.it.nwu.edu/~pib/
catindiv.htm

This comprehensive list of individual cat pages boggles the
mind. You could spend an entire
day just trying to wade—or
paw—through them.

CAT-RELATED NEWSGROUPS

Newsgroups are a kind of electronic bulletin board where folks go to discuss a wide range of topics, from child-rearing to Karl Malden's nose. Many groups are silly, while some are infinitely helpful. Usenet, a facet of the Internet, is a collection of newsgroups. To access Usenet, you'll need a "newsreader," incorporated into most browsers. Another way to access newsgroups is to go to http://www/dejanews.com. Here is a list of groups relating to our friend, the cat:

rec.pets.cats
rec.pets.cats.anecdotes
rec.pets.cats.health+behavior
rec.pets.cats.misc
rec.pets.cats.rescue